MILTON MELTZER

Carl Sandburg

A BIOGRAPHY

Twenty-First Century Books • Brookfield, Connecticut

BY MILTON MELTZER

Langston Hughes: A Biography

*Food: How We Hunt and Gather It, How We Grow and Eat It,
How We Buy and Sell It, How We Preserve and Waste It, and How
Some Have Too Much and Others Have Too Little of It*

Ten Queens: Portraits of Women of Power

Weapons and Warfare: From Stone Age to Space Age

Piracy and Plunder: A Murderous Business

The Many Lives of Andrew Carnegie

Witchcraft and Witch Hunts

≈≈≈

Cover photograph courtesy of UPI/Corbis-Bettmann

Photographs courtesy of Carl Sandburg Collection,
University of Illinois Library: pp. 4, 9 (both), 16, 19, 34, 38, 45, 53, 59, 71, 77, 81, 102,
110, 119, 127, 130; © Stock Montage: p. 30; Rare Book Room, University of Illinois
Library: p. 36; Clifton Waller Barrett Library, Special Collections Department, University
of Virginia Library: p. 51; Carl Sandburg State Historic Site, Galesburg, Illinois: p. 139.

Library of Congress Cataloging-in-Publication Data
Meltzer, Milton, 1915–
Carl Sandburg : a biography / by Milton Meltzer
p   cm.
Includes biographical references and index.
Summary: A biography of the poet who became known for his
ability to speak to the common people, by shaping out of the plain
English of ordinary Americans the voice of their vast experience.
ISBN 0-7613-1364-8 (lib. bdg.)
1. Sandburg, Carl 1878-1967—Juvenile literature.   2. Poets, American—20th century—
Biography—Juvenile literature.   3. Biographers—United States—Biography—Juvenile
literature. {1. Sandburg, Carl, 1878-1967. 2. Poets, American.}   I. Title.
PS3537.A618Z775   1999   811'.52—dc21 {B}   98-46373   CIP   AC

Published by Twenty-First Century Books
A Division of The Millbrook Press, Inc.
2 Old New Milford Road, Brookfield, Connecticut 06804
Visit us on our Website:
www.millbrookpress.com

CONTENTS

FOREWORD

Who doesn't know this poem?

FOG
The fog comes
on little cat feet.
It sits looking
over harbor and city
on silent haunches
and then moves on.

That twenty-one word poem is read and recited and memorized in schools just about everywhere. But what about Carl Sandburg, the poet who wrote it? How much do you know about him?

Maybe you think poets are a special kind of human—sensitive, delicate, remote from everyday life, living in a loftier realm than the rest of us, making out of language a fine-spun dream. We say, "He looks like a poet," or "She looks like a poet" when we see someone with refined features, dreamy eyes, an out-of-this-world air.

But poets come in all shapes and sizes and colors and personalities. And some lead tough, brawling lives, getting into trouble, suffering disasters, gaining brief fame, losing it, dying unknown—maybe to be remembered long after the grave.

Carl Sandburg is one of the poets who has never been forgotten. He lived a long time, eighty-nine years (1878–1967), and, reaching midlife, became so celebrated that prizes and honors and rich rewards were showered upon him almost yearly. He was esteemed not only as a poet, but as a biographer of Abraham Lincoln (in six volumes!), as a journalist, and as a performer. He traveled into every corner of America reading his poems to eager audiences and singing folksongs as he accompanied himself on his guitar. Someone who heard him perform wrote: "One comes away with the feeling that Sandburg himself, with his shaggy gray head and pugnosed Swedish face and whimsical loveableness, *was* poetry."

He was the son of an immigrant Swede, a railroad worker who earned $35 a month. Young Carl never went to high school, and for years and years and years to earn a living he set his hand to a vast variety of jobs—newsboy, shoeshine boy, milkman, dishwasher, farm laborer, and lots more, including his time as a union man and a socialist organizer.

It's hard to think of many other poets who lived a working-class life, and shaped out of the plain English of ordinary Americans the voice of their vast experience.

This is his story.

CHAPTER

1

A Kind of Joy

**ARL WAS ONLY TEN** when a strike broke out on the railroad his father worked for. August Sandburg was a blacksmith in the repair shop. The engineers who drove the locomotives wanted better pay and shorter hours. They had struck when the company wouldn't meet their demands. Instead, the bosses brought in nonunion workers to break the strike. When the union men, wild with anger, confronted the scabs, one of the striking engineers was shot dead. The union claimed it was done by a Pinkerton, one of the private detectives hired by the railroad to protect the scabs and smash the union. On his way to school the next day, Carl saw the spot where the engineer had fallen on the sidewalk. His blood had turned dry and rusty on the wooden board.

That strike was lost. Why was the boy all for the strikers and against the railroad? Maybe because Carl knew some of the men and liked them. But young as he was he saw the railroad "as a big inhuman Something that refused to recognize and deal with the engineers who in all weathers took their locomotives out along the rails, hoping to pull through without a collision or a slide down an embankment."

Even at ten Carl was already a partisan. He took sides, he seemed to know what was right and what was wrong, what was fair and what was not. He took, he said, "a kind of joy in the complete justice of the cause of the strikers."

Carl's father, August Sandburg, was an immigrant, part of a new wave of people rolling in from the far-off corners of Europe. They came to escape conscription and war, find decent wages and equality, know freedom and justice for the first time. But when they reached America, immigrants often found their golden dreams turned into nightmares.

August Sandburg had come in steerage from Sweden in 1870 or 1871. He, too, hoped to find a better life than the harsh toil of

August and Clara Sandburg, Swedish immigrants, were the parents of seven childen. Carl was their second child and first son.

his peasant family at home. But what he found in Galesburg, Illinois, a prairie town in the upper Midwest, was hardly better. A job, yes, on the Chicago, Burlington and Quincy Railroad. But it demanded twelve hours a day, six days a week, for very low pay and no vacations.

In Illinois, August met Clara Anderson, a hotel maid fresh from Sweden, bright with the same golden hopes. They married and settled into a three-room cottage close by the roundhouse where August worked as a blacksmith's helper. That was the end of their travels, for they would always stay close to home. They had seven children; Carl was their second child and first son.

There were lots of other Swedes in Galesburg, many of them laborers on the railroad. They came at a time when the nation's industrial life had been transformed by the Civil War. To meet the needs of that struggle, old factories were remade and giant new ones sprang up, using faster and better methods of production. Thousands of miles of railroads and of telegraph wires laced the country together.

Everything was changing. People born into a nation of farmers, independent craftsmen, and small manufacturers had lived largely on the countryside. But now a nation of great capitalists and big factories was massing wage earners in the cities. Right here in Galesburg, George W. Brown, a farm boy turned carpenter, had invented a machine to plant corn. His factory was turning out thousands of cornplanters during the war years, increasing food production to help the North win the war. Hundreds of men worked for him, and by the time Carl was born, Mr. Brown was the town mayor.

As immigrants tend to wherever they settle, the Swedes in Galesburg clung together in their own neighborhoods, churches, and lodges, and got their news from a Swedish-language paper. That degree of separation from the larger community made young Carl feel he was different, not really American. Even "Carl" sounded foreign to him, and he began to call himself "Charles."

Yet there were other minorities in town: many Irish, some Italians, Chinese, and many African Americans who had come north on the Underground Railroad and stayed on amid the pioneers who had created the prairie town in 1837. By the time of Carl's birth, Galesburg's 18,000 people made it the biggest city in Knox County. A fourth of its population held jobs of one kind or another on the railroads. For Galesburg was a railroad hub, which meant trains were constantly crossing, heading east or west with heavy loads of freight.

When Carl was three, the family was able to buy a ten-room house, renting out the extra space. Clever with hand and tool, August Sandburg used every kind of skill to repair or improve his property. Carl and the other sons helped, always fearful of displeasing August, for breaking or spoiling or neglecting something might bring a heavy clop on the head.

Carl's mother, Clara, was a lovely, gentle woman, less scarred by years of the long economic depression that had begun in 1873. It was one of America's worst crises, throwing every fifth worker out of a job. At least ten million people had gone hungry, with most getting no public relief. Many families, including the Sandburgs, had a hard time staying afloat until the crisis ended.

No wonder August Sandburg was always worrying about money. He denied himself much, smoking only one five-cent cigar a month, wearing his only suit till it almost fell apart. Smile? Laugh? Sing? He was too tired after the long day at the forge, yet would find things that needed doing till bedtime. The children were never read to or talked to, never felt an affectionate pat or heard a sweet word. And a kiss seemed beyond his nature.

The very first book Carl remembered seeing was the family Bible. One winter night, when he was four, he heard his father reading aloud to his mother. What was that big heavy thing his father was holding? And why was he saying those strange words? The next day he went to the bureau where the Bible lay on top, and carried it to the nearby window so he could see it better. What did those black marks on white paper mean? How could they be words your eyes could pick up and change into words your tongue could speak? He asked his mother for help. She put her finger on one word, and then on another, and another, and slowly spoke the words the black marks signified. The child had a glimmer of understanding. Wait, his mother said, you'll soon be going to school where they'll teach you to read.

And they did. He caught on fast. He found what good friends books could be. Stories about the American Revolution thrilled him—the farmers at Lexington shooting from behind stone walls at the British Redcoats, the troops ragged and starving that winter at Valley Forge, Tom Paine writing "These are the times that try men's souls," the victorious General Washington saying good-bye to his officers at Fraunce's Tavern . . . He loved the illustrations, too, but was puzzled that the books told you who the author was, but didn't bother to mention the artist.

What was happening in the larger world in 1878, the year Carl Sandburg was born?

- The first regular telephone line was opened, in New Haven, Connecticut.
- Thomas Edison patented his new device, the phonograph, and made the first recording to be played on it. It was "Mary Had a Little Lamb."
- In England, Gilbert and Sullivan presented their new musical, *HMS Pinafore*.
- In London, electrical street lighting was introduced.
- In America, the first bicycle was manufactured. It was called "wheels."
- The population of the United States was about 50 million. (Today it is more than five times that much.)

August Sandburg had learned to read as a boy in Sweden, but he never learned to write. He had little use for words; they held no mystery or charm for him, Carl recalled. But Carl's mother shared her son's love for books and words. Twice she dared defy August's tightfistedness by buying two books from a traveling salesman, both of them fat encyclopedias whose news of the great big world Carl delighted in.

Carl looked like a combination of his mother and father. He had thick brown hair and hazel eyes that changed color under different lights. His body was strong; he moved gracefully like a natural athlete. Though he felt shy on the inside, his friendly grin came easily.

When he was in the second grade, his teacher, Miss Maggie Mullen, recognized his love for language and encouraged him to read. The biographies of famous men (few authors chose to write about women in those days) were his favorite. When he was eight, Ulysses S. Grant, the Union Army leader and former President, died, and Galesburg honored the dead hero with a funeral parade. Carl watched the Union veterans from atop his father's shoulders. Like Grant, August was a strong Republican, and took his boy to political rallies. But that allegiance faded early; Carl would move to the left, giving his father another reason to be angry at him.

At eleven, Carl entered the fifth grade and met another cherished teacher, Miss Lottie Goldquist. He was an A student in all his classes—geography, arithmetic, English. Miss Goldquist told her class about Eugene Field, a poet who had gone to Knox College right there in Galesburg. He wrote folk poetry, weaving in people's customs and talk, and was often very funny. She read Field's "Little Boy Blue" to the class. Good, she said, but I like even more Longfellow's "The Psalm of Life." For years afterward Carl would recite to himself some of the lines from "The Psalm," for they had music and hope in them.

It could have been a very happy year if his father hadn't suffered a financial loss in a complex deal involving property he had invested in. It saddled him with a debt of about $800, an enormous burden for a man with seven children who earned about $1.40 a day. The sum he owed was almost double his annual earnings. He couldn't stop brooding over it. He would sink into long silences and drive himself harder at work, less able than ever to offer the affection his children hungered for.

What could a boy do? Carl found an after-school job to help out. He swept the floor and cleaned the spittoons in the office of a real-estate firm—pay: twenty-five cents a week. It was the first of many jobs he would have while growing up.

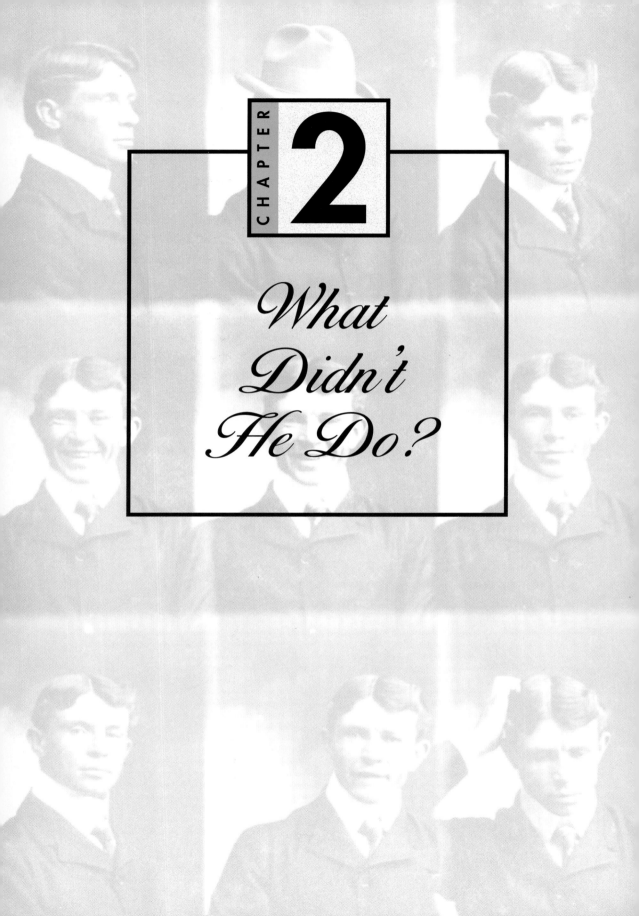

CHAPTER

2

What Didn't He Do?

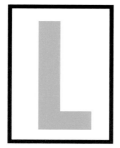**IFE IN GALESBURG** wasn't all school and nothing else. On the street Carl and his friends spun tops, played mumblety-peg, baseball, duck-on-a-rock. The boys enjoyed watching the track-and-field sports on the campuses of the two local colleges, Knox and Lombard. And later, in the streets, they set up their own competitive events—the 50-yard and the 100-yard dash, the mile run, the broad jump and high jump, and even the pole vault.

Summers they frolicked in a swimming hole they called the "Root." A tree had been knocked down in a storm and its huge root fell across a creek, making a dam with water almost up to the belly button.

But one afternoon the boys decided not to walk out of town to the Root. Instead, they stripped and jumped buck-naked into a small neighborhood pond. The police happened to go by, tossed them all into the patrol wagon, and herded them into a cell crowded with drunks. Finally a justice of the peace showed up and let them off with a short sermon, and on the promise they'd not swim naked again within the town limits. Carl's folks weren't angry at him when he got home. After all, hadn't they seen him born naked? And hadn't they soaped him naked in the laundry tub? They thought the police had been silly.

At band concerts on the public square Friday nights the boys had lots of fun listening to the music and looking at the girls as they strolled around. After, everyone moved to the drugstore for ice-cream sodas. The YMCA was another hangout. There Carl learned to play chess, and built a reputation at checkers. He even beat the town champ a few times.

Maybe twice a month the teenage crowd ran their own dance. Each boy and girl paid a quarter, for which they rented a hall, hired two fiddlers, and danced the waltz and the two-step. It gave a shy fellow the opportunity to get to know smooth-dancing girls with pretty faces.

15

Twelve-year-old Carl Sandburg (first row left) and his
confirmation class at Elim Lutheran Church, Galesburg, 1891

Carl got his first chance to perform for an audience when he
joined a Sunday school class. The teachers were students at Knox
College. Besides reading the Bible together, on some evenings
they put on shows for grownups and children. Carl was in a quartet and remembered singing the Negro spiritual, "Don't Take the
Left-Hand Road."

In a one-act play he acted the part of a tramp. Once he entered
a declamation contest. The eight boys and girls competing for the
prize of a silver medal had to choose their pieces from a book that

contained only speeches against the evils of alcohol. Carl chose the shortest one to memorize. When his turn came, he walked to the front of the platform and began spouting, very glad that he wouldn't have to stand there long. But near the middle his mind suddenly went blank. Oh God, what were the next words? A long, long silence as everyone stared at him. Then suddenly a gear shifted in his head and the right words came out of his mouth. But of course he didn't win the prize. Still, wasn't this a good year? For the first time he'd acted in a play, made a public speech, and sang for an audience.

Carl always liked to sing. One of his friends was Willis Calkins, who played the banjo and knew lots of popular songs, minstrel tunes, and old ballads. He showed Carl the chords and taught him how to accompany songs. In a pawnshop Carl bought a two-dollar banjo and took a few twenty-five-cent lessons. It helped when a music teacher came to his school once a week, handed out a book of songs, and took the class through every one of them.

One of Carl's favorite hangouts was the back room of a cigar store. Julius Schultz, the owner, enjoyed having the kids around, noisy as they were. Four of them formed a quartet, with Carl singing bass. They harmonized on "Swanee River," "Carry Me Back to Old Virginia," and lots of other popular songs. Carl often heard the tunes in the Auditorium, when Broadway shows on tour reached Galesburg.

The Auditorium was one of the places where Carl could earn some money while still at school. He worked as a supernumerary, one of the band of local boys who were hired to make noise backstage or below stage when the script called for such sounds, or to help stagehands shift scenes. Sometimes he worked high above the stage in the "flies," hauling up a curtain or pulling one down by the ropes—pay: ten cents a night.

He saw many a famous person that way. World champion boxers like John L. Sullivan and Jim Corbett made extra money in plays tailored to display their brawn. Leading actors such as Joe Jefferson and James O'Neill toured the country for decades in old melodramas or comedies the audiences never seemed to tire of.

And of course there were the endless dramatic variations on Harriet Beecher Stowe's novel, *Uncle Tom's Cabin.* The African explorer Henry M. Stanley and the Arctic explorer Fridtjof Nansen showed up on the Galesburg stage, too.

In 1892, Carl turned fourteen, and his schooling ended. His older sister Mary was allowed to attend high school, but August Sandburg felt the family needed whatever money Carl might earn. Not unusual then, for many students never went beyond grade school. They understood why, for it was constantly drilled into them that "Money talks. Even when it stinks, it talks." Not to have any was a disaster, and most people thought it was your own fault if you were poor.

So Carl went from one job to another—some part-time, some full-time, some now-and-then. None paid much, but whatever it was, the family needed it. He distributed handbills, part of a crew of boys who worked from 8 A.M. to 6 P.M., walking from door to door in all weather, stuffing circulars under doormats or leaving them on the steps, for twenty-five cents a day. He kept his old after-school newspaper route, earning a dollar a week delivering not only the local paper but the Chicago papers. Glancing through them he began to learn much about what was going on in the wider world.

It's hard to think of something Carl didn't do in those years when others were in high school. He spaded gardens. He cleaned bricks when houses were torn down. At harvest time, for twenty-five cents a day he carried water to the men in the fields. He worked as a porter in a hotel's barbershop, and shined shoes for a nickel.

One summer he worked at the boathouse on a lake, helping people into the rowboats and selling ice cream, candy, and sodas at the refreshment stand. One winter he spent two weeks in freezing weather harvesting ice on the lake all night long for his highest pay thus far, $1.25 a night.

Maybe I should try to master a trade, he thought. A tinsmith took him on, but Carl quit when the man was often too drunk to show up. Then he tried the potter's trade, only to lose out when the pottery burned down. And there was the summer he washed

Carl, at fifteen, looks like the picture of prosperity dressed for his work as a hotel barbershop porter, but in actuality this was just one of many menial jobs he held because his family was too poor to allow him to attend high school. They needed his income.

bottles in a bottling works, from seven in the morning till six at night. You could drink all the soda pop you wanted, which was just the trouble, for Carl downed so much of it he ended up with a diarrhea that knocked him and the job out.

Then came a job that lasted much longer than all the others. It was with a dairy farm two miles out of town. He walked there, and walked back, too, saving a nickel carfare each way. He put in seven days a week, from 7 A.M. to 1 P.M. as the milkman's helper, carrying the heavy cans of milk to people's doors, and filling their empty pails.

Then one day, his two little brothers, Emil and Fred, came down with fevers that rapidly grew worse. Diphtheria, the doctor announced, a killer disease. Within three days both boys were dead. Atop his heavy old debt, August now had to bear the costs of the doctor, the undertaker, the caskets, the cemetery plot. It was lucky Carl was earning $12 a month.

That winter—bitter with the loss of his brothers, bitter with unrelenting snow and ice—Carl kept at his milk route, his feet freezing, unable to spare a dollar for overshoes, or two dollars for warm felt boots.

CHAPTER **3**

*Free for
What?
Free for
Whom?*

**FEW MONTHS** after Emil and Fred died, Mrs. Sandburg had a baby girl—new life in the midst of the grief the family suffered. The year 1893 saw the onset of another depression. When it began, there were 12.5 million families in the United States. Of these, 11 million had an average income of $350 a year. The richest 1 percent of the country enjoyed wealth greater than the total of the remaining 99 percent. Businesses failed, stores closed, factories laid off many workers. In those hard times the railroad cut Carl's father to four days work a week, reducing his monthly paycheck to less than $16. So the $12 a month Carl got on the milk route was a godsend to the family.

"We're not rich and we're not poor," the young Carl used to tell himself. They were just on the boundary line of poor. If Carl had lost his job, or his father had been laid off, the family would have plunged into a bottomless pit. Only those who have lived on that terribly thin edge can understand what it's like.

Carl grew closer to his sister Mary. About to graduate high school, she planned to become a teacher. She helped prepare herself by teaching her brother Carl. She shared novels with him—Walter Scott's *Ivanhoe* and Nathaniel Hawthorne's *The Scarlet Letter*—and lent him her big textbook on how American government worked.

But did it really work the way the textbook said? Carl began to have his doubts when he talked about it with his friend John Sjodin. A few years older than Carl, John had worked in a department store in Chicago, that great sprawling city Carl yearned to visit. John's father, a skilled tailor, was "the first real radical I knew as a boy," Carl said. A proud craftsman, Mr. Sjodin talked about building a new society, where no man would cringe before another. He was a socialist who despised "the plutocrats who rob the poor."

Like his father, young John was all for political action against the big corporations who ran the country, as he saw it. He talked to Carl about the time when the aroused working people would rise up and gain political power, eliminating the gross extremes between rich and poor.

Carl liked him. He didn't think John could ever lead a mob or incite a riot. No, he had "a reverence for life and said many a time that he couldn't hate a millionaire, and most of the rich were sorry fools who didn't know what to do with their money except to put it to work to make more money."

What John did for Carl was to start him thinking for himself. Just because something is printed in a newspaper or a book does not mean it's true. Ask questions! Take nothing for granted! Look for the facts! He made Carl want to know a lot more about what was going on in his America.

This was the year that Carl got his chance to see Chicago. He was eighteen now, yet had never been more than fifty miles from home. After much pleading, his father gave in and secured a rail-road pass for his son. He went off with $1.50 to carry him through a three-day holiday. A million people lived in the great city. It was like nothing he had experienced before. He could not know it then, but it was here that he would one day make his name as a journalist and poet.

He stayed in a cheap hotel John Sjodin had told him of, ate at a free-lunch saloon, walked miles and miles of streets, got his first look at endless Lake Michigan, and went to vaudeville shows two nights running. He searched out Haymarket Square, where in 1886 a bomb had exploded, killing ten policemen—a tragedy for which several radicals were convicted on falsified evidence and sentenced to death.

Back home in Galesburg, Carl felt the town painfully dull and infinitely smaller after the excitement and vitality of Chicago. Will I ever escape jobs that lead nowhere? Am I capable of something better?

This was 1896, an election year, and everyone was wondering who would be the next president. Carl began to follow politics, although he wouldn't be able to vote for another three years. The depression that had begun in 1893 was still hurting badly. And those who suffered most were all for the Democratic candidate, young and handsome William Jennings Bryan, newspaper editor and Congressman. He had risen in a new party, the Populist or People's Party. It wanted to make America over. Farmers whose lives had been made miserable by the railroads, the mortgage companies, the trusts, and the middlemen were joined by workers and the poor and unemployed who felt government had done nothing for them.

The Democrats, seeing Bryan's great popularity, put him on their ticket. William C. McKinley was the candidate of big business on the Republican ticket. Bryan did well, getting the biggest Democratic vote in history. But not enough to beat McKinley.

The candidacy of a Populist like Bryan scared the "respectable" people who voted Republican. They remembered the Haymarket bombing. And the time in 1892 when a battle between 300 armed Pinkerton guards and the workers at Andrew Carnegie's Homestead steel mill had resulted in ten men killed and seventy wounded. On top of that had come the panic of 1893 and the breadlines. And then, in the next year, during a strike by the Pullman railway workers, federal troops were sent in to smash the union. Some said a revolution was around the corner.

Reading in the papers about all these terrible events made Carl wonder about the America he was part of. Everyone, in Galesburg and all over the country, lived under the Stars and Stripes. But what did citizenship mean? That men were willing to die for it, he knew. Why? "When they say it is a free country, they mean free for what and free for whom? And what is freedom?"

4

Hobo
and
Soldier

I **N 1897, CARL TURNED NINETEEN.** He didn't think he was much for looks. But others saw him as handsome. He had grown tall and lean. A wave of dark hair fell over his high forehead, a charming look he would always have.

Late that June he decided he had had enough of Galesburg. He must get away, see more of America and more of life. Mama and Papa didn't like it, but they didn't try to stop him. This time he left with $3.75 in cash. As a freight train pulled out of the station, he ran alongside and leaped into a boxcar. When the train crossed the Mississippi and slowed down in Iowa, he jumped out. It was the first time he had touched soil outside Illinois.

He was part of an army of hundreds of thousands of wanderers, young and old. Since the Civil War there had always been migrants moving west, hopping aboard freight trains; some searched for work, some were determined never to work, but to live by begging or stealing. Tramps, they were called, or hoboes, or bums. Mostly they followed the railroad lines, traveling illegally, in danger of being thrown off or beaten up or jailed.

Many were maimed or killed in railroad accidents. About 6,000 were reported injured in 1897 alone. Carl himself narrowly escaped death when riding close to Denver. Unable to find an empty boxcar, he rode the bumpers late one night. His feet were on the bumpers between two cars, and his hands clung to a brake rod in case his feet should slip off. Suddenly he realized he had fallen asleep. If his hands had loosened he would have toppled under the moving train. He kept punching his head to stay awake until the train stopped and he could jump off. What a stupid, reckless fool he had been! Thank God, thank God, he kept muttering, I've made it alive. . . .

He met all kinds of men, and some women, too, in the boxcars or the hobo jungles—those patches of trees where the migrants holed up for a while. Sometimes he walked house to house in a town, knocking on doors to ask for odd jobs in return for a meal. He found if he said he was trying to earn money for college, people were more likely to be kind. But he hadn't the slightest idea of whether, or how, or when, or where he would go to college.

For nearly four months Carl made his way west. He cooked at lunch counters, worked on a railway section gang, washed dishes, harvested hay, threshed wheat. But he got much more than a meal or a dollar from the experience. As he recalled later:

> I was meeting fellow travelers and fellow Americans. What they were doing to my heart and mind, my personality, I couldn't say then nor later and be certain. I was getting a deeper self-respect than I had had in Galesburg, so much I knew. . . . A way deep in my heart now I had hope as never before. Struggles lay ahead, I was sure, but whatever they were I would not be afraid of them.

The newspapers said the country was pulling out of hard times. True, more factories were running full tilt and prosperity seemed to be returning. But many people were still out of work, and Carl kept running into men who'd left home seeking jobs elsewhere, anywhere.

For the first time he began to keep a journal. In it he recorded the stories the hoboes told, the songs they sang, the vivid language they spoke. Their faces, their gestures, their moods, their fears and loves and hates entered his mind and moved his heart. The journal was a storehouse crammed with treasures that would one day enrich his poetry and prose.

As fall came on, Carl grew tired of life on the road and a little homesick for family and friends in Galesburg. From the Rockies, he worked his way back east riding the rails. In Nebraska, a lawyer for whom he chopped wood gave him a gray woolen suit—used, but by far the best Carl had ever owned. That night the empty boxcar on a siding that he and four other hoboes tried to sleep in proved so cold they walked to the town jail where a marshal let them sleep on a cell floor till morning.

He reached home on October 15 to be hugged and kissed by his mother. He found a job on a dairy farm, driving the milk wagon three miles into town to make deliveries. As the horse plodded the slow miles to and fro, Carl studied a lecture series prepared by professors and serialized in a Chicago paper.

In January he marked his twentieth birthday. Restless again, he quit the dairy and apprenticed himself to a Swedish house painter. It meant a ten-hour day, six days a week. Another boring job, scraping off old paint and sandpapering wood to prepare for painting.

Then came a great shock to the country. On February 15, 1898, the U.S. battleship *Maine* exploded in the harbor of Havana, Cuba. The toll was heavy: 266 of the 354 officers and men on board were killed. How had it happened? Who or what was to blame?

Like everyone else, Carl was excited by the terrible news. What was our battleship doing in Cuban waters? American business had made large investments in the island, seeking high profits from cheap labor, and farmers did well exporting food to Cuba. Investors wanted a peaceful Cuba to ensure continued prosperity.

But some of the powerful government figures had long wanted more. They wanted to reshape American foreign policy, to build up the Navy so that the United States would become dominant throughout the Western Hemisphere.

Cuba had been a Spanish possession since Columbus claimed it for Spain in 1492. In 1895 a movement to overthrow Spanish rule began that laid waste to the countryside and cost many lives on both sides. To weaken the guerrilla forces the Spanish commander, General Weyler, had imprisoned many women and children in concentration camps, where hundreds died of starvation and disease.

News of the horror of the camps stirred sympathy in the United States for the rebels' cause. Many Americans wished to end the suffering of the Cuban people and help them gain their independence. At the same time, halfway around the world, another revolt had erupted against Spanish rule—in the Philippines, which had been claimed for Spain back in 1571, when Magellan's fleet had landed there.

Congressmen and cabinet members urged President McKinley to take control of the Philippines as a springboard into Asian markets if the United States went to war with Spain to end the trouble in Cuba. Washington made proposals to Spain for solving the crisis that would bring the United States economic and strategic gains, and the President threatened military intervention if his proposals were not accepted. In the first months of 1898, as the crisis mounted, McKinley sent the battleship *Maine* to Havana to protect, he said, American life and property. Seven days later the *Maine* blew up.

The American press, seeking sensations to sell papers in a highly competitive market, didn't wait for a careful investigation of the disaster. Headlines screamed "Foul Play!" War fever swept the nation under the slogan of "Remember the *Maine!*" Giving in to public pressure, Congress declared war on Spain. (Not until the 1970s did a U.S. Navy Department investigation of the disaster conclude that the *Maine* was blown up when heat from a fire in a coal bunker adjacent to the reserve magazine of gunpowder ignited it.)

On April 26, two days after war was declared, Carl joined Company C of the Sixth Infantry Regiment, Illinois volunteers. His enlistment papers said he was "21 years of age, 5 feet ten inches high, ruddy complexion, grey eyes, brown hair, and by occupation a painter." (He would not be twenty-one for another ten months.) His mother wept at the station as his company boarded a train to go off to war.

They got off at Springfield, the state capital, and went into training—drill with a rifle, the manual of arms. Ten days later they were moved to Virginia, where they drilled until the end of June. Carl got to know the men in his company. About a dozen were students from the Galesburg colleges, Knox or Lombard, and another twenty were farm boys. Like himself, they had volunteered to find adventure, to test themselves in danger, to see what hardships they could stand. A "mystic love of country" was there, too, to a degree. Some talked of escaping from the dull monotonous round of everyday life back home.

Then in July they were moved to Charleston, South Carolina. There they boarded a big freighter that had been converted into a troopship, and six days later arrived in Guantanamo Bay, Cuba,

For Carl Sandburg, who would become a noted journalist as well as poet, the reporting of the Spanish-American War might have been a great lesson—in what *not* to do. History students may recall the telegraphed exchange between William Randolph Hearst, publisher of the *New York Journal*, and Frederick Remington, the great illustrator of the American frontier. Hearst had sent the artist to Cuba to report on the uprising against the Spanish.

"There will be no war; I wish to return," Remington wired. "Stay where you are!" Hearst told him. "You furnish the pictures. I'll furnish the war."

And so Hearst did, with scary headlines and inaccurate articles that heated up the American conflict with Spain. In the rush to print, Hearst and other papers published unconfirmed reports, and even wholly faked ones. They placed Havana datelines on stories invented by men on the New York desk. Such "journalism" reached its climax with the sensationalistic coverage of the sinking of the battleship *Maine*.

where battleships, cruisers, and torpedo boats lay at anchor. In the morning their colonel went ashore; he returned with the news that Santiago, the big stronghold of the Spanish, had been captured. It meant the war was over.

It had lasted only a hundred days. It was the shortest and easiest of all American wars, totally one-sided. Spain was then at the lowest point of two centuries of decline. The Spaniards were so outmanned and outgunned that there was never any doubt about the outcome. It was virtually a walkover. It cost the United States 385 killed in battle and 2,061 dead for "other causes," mostly from yellow fever.

As Spain gave up Cuba, America occupied the island and later got from Spain the Caribbean island of Puerto Rico, the Pacific island of Guam, and all the Philippines.

The news of Santiago's fall pleased many of Carl's company, but some were disappointed to miss out on combat. After a few days at anchor, their ship sailed to Puerto Rico, where some skirmishing was still breaking out. But Carl's company saw no action there, either.

Back to the transport to sail off to New York. Many of the men had lost much weight; Carl dropped to 130 pounds. In New York they took a train to Springfield, where their discharge papers were given them. Then the short ride to Galesburg, arriving on September 21.

They had been gone only five months. A big crowd greeted them at the station, the Sandburgs among them, laughing and waving.

The next day at home, Carl's father, proud of his son, gave him a fierce handshake. His shopmates had often asked him how his boy was doing away at war. It made August Sandburg, the Swedish immigrant, feel that now, surely, he was truly an American citizen. Carl had received about a hundred dollars in mustering-out pay; he gave his father half of it.

At night in their room, Carl's brother Mart teased him. Last year you were a hobo, he said, and this year a soldier. What'll come next?

"Maybe I'll go to college."

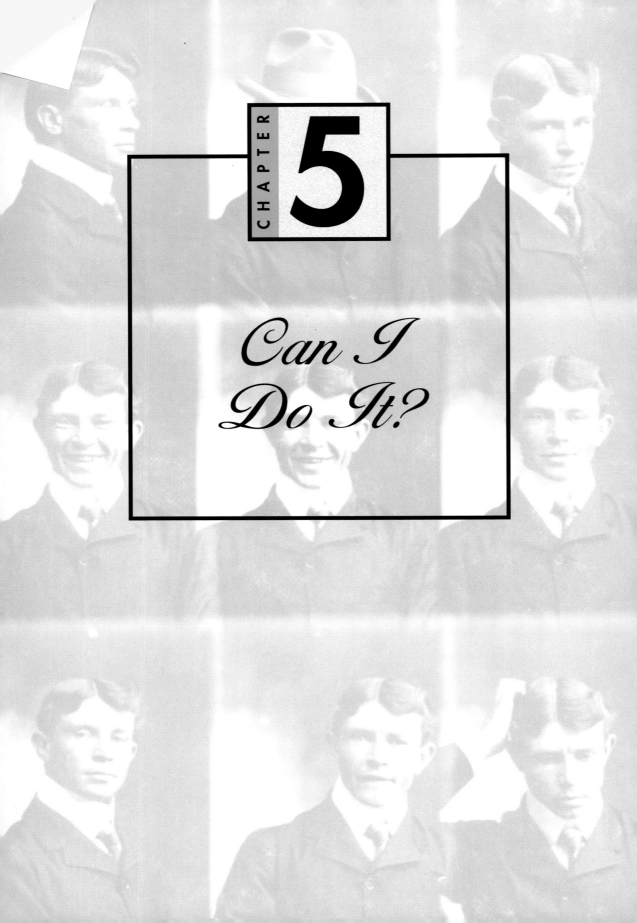

CHAPTER

5

Can I Do It?

SOMETIMES THE MOST UNEXPECTED events can change your life—a chance meeting, a casual conversation, a small item in a newspaper, a paragraph in a book. It happens to nearly all of us; it happened to Carl.

He never expected to go to college. Even though there were two right there in Galesburg. How could he enter college when he hadn't gone to high school? And when his folks couldn't spare a dollar for it?

What opened the door was a conversation with a soldier in his company as they were sailing to Cuba. George had just finished his freshman year at Lombard College when he volunteered for service. How about you, Carl, he'd asked. Would you go if you got free tuition? Well, why not? Carl said. When he got home, he found that Lombard was admitting veterans tuition-free. Because he didn't have a high school diploma, he'd have to take some preparatory courses as well as the regular college courses.

So he enrolled as a special student, signing up for Latin, English, chemistry, drama, and public speaking. He was going to get an education. He remembered his grade school teacher, Miss Goldquist, had said, "You can never get enough of it!" He still needed to earn money to support himself and help his family. A friend told him of a job at a fire station as "call man." It paid ten dollars a month. Whenever there was a fire, a piercing whistle blew and he would have to hustle out of class to jump aboard his bike and rush to the fire. The Lombard professors knew of his job, and didn't mind.

He slept on the second floor of the fire station, with fifteen other men. When the alarm bell rang at night, they pulled on their pants, slid down the brass pole, and hopped on the fire wagon.

About this time August Sandburg sold the family's big old house for a profit, and moved the family into another one, just across the street. August was still a blacksmith's helper, at 14 cents an hour. But his frugality, the renting out of rooms, the doing

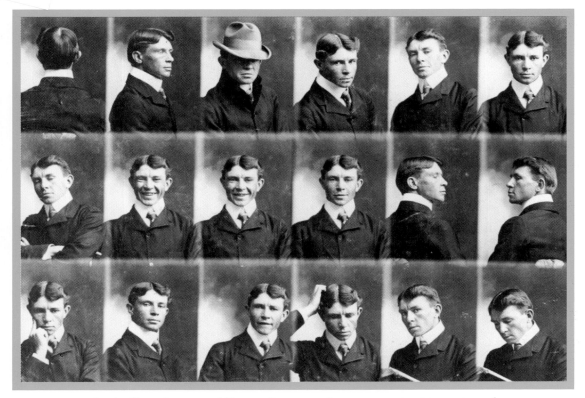

Carl offered many different faces to the camera in this series of photos believed to have been taken around his twenty-first birthday. This was the time when the boy who had drifted through dozens of jobs became a college man, and the fragments of his life began to come together as his writing talent emerged.

of his own repairs, had paid off. Now maybe they were middle class? Or almost? Mart helped his father with odd jobs. Carl, too, after class and in between fires, pitched in. A little older and wiser now, he realized his father loved to work for the sake of work itself. He took pride in creating something, shaping it with his own brain and hands. Carl, too, would know that wonderful feeling when he discovered the work he was truly meant for.

Toward the end of his first year at Lombard, Carl learned that the army unit he had served in was entitled to a cadetship at West

Point, the U.S. Military Academy. And he had been chosen! But he had to pass a written entry exam first. He failed the math test, went back to Lombard, and in September 1899 began his sophomore year.

Lombard was somewhat like Temple in Philadelphia or City College in New York. These colleges were meant to give the children of the working class a chance to better themselves. Studying the cultures of their own and other societies and being exposed to the influence of good professors could change their lives, open new avenues to careers, raise the possibility they might make some important contribution to the community.

Lombard had graduated its first class—four boys and two girls—in 1856. Two years later, Lombard students welcomed Abe Lincoln, "Champion of Liberty," when as candidate for the U.S. Senate he came to Galesburg for one of the famous debates with Stephen A. Douglas. Now, fifty years later, the campus covered four city blocks. It had 175 students, and a faculty of nineteen.

Carl plunged headlong into college life, trying almost everything offered. He captained the basketball team, and he sang with the glee club. He joined the debating society and won a prize for an oration. In his senior year he was made editor-in-chief of *The Lombard Review*, the college paper.

While keeping up with his studies and extracurricular activities, he still managed to handle odd jobs on campus or in town. He earned some money as janitor of the college gym and a bit more ringing the college bell to open and close class periods. He also knocked on nearby farm doors to sell stereoscopic slides.

His earnings, small as they were, were added to sister Mary's schoolteacher salary of $30 a month. It made his father less fretful about a son spending four years studying. As for his mother, she kept saying, "You do the best you can, and maybe you make a name for yourself."

The strongest and most lasting influence on Carl at Lombard was Professor Philip Green Wright. A multitalented man, he taught not only English but economics, mathematics, and astronomy. (His father, Elizur Wright, had been a noted abolitionist.)

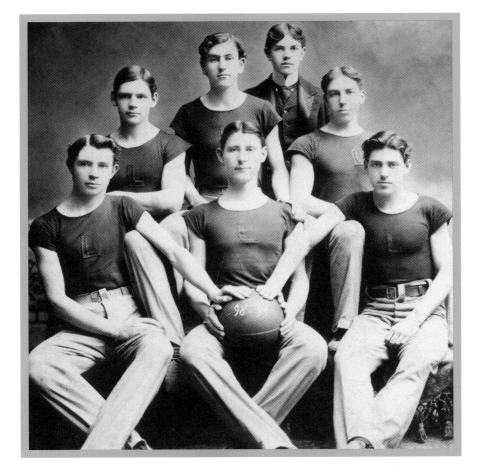

Carl, shown in the front row left, loved basketball and was the captain of the Lombard team. He later said, "Basketball had a fascination for me, and during the four years I never thought of quitting the game."

On his own time, Philip Wright was a poet, a printer, a book-binder, an editor, "a genius and a marvel," Carl said. He became a "fine and dear friend, a deeply beloved teacher." When a boy or girl finds such a teacher, whether in school or college, it is a godsend.

Wright soon saw that in Carl he had a student of rare talent and great promise. He asked Carl and two others to come to his home Sunday afternoons to read and discuss what each had written during the week. "The Poor Writers Club," as they called them-selves, not only criticized their own work but read aloud such eminent authors as Mark Twain, Rudyard Kipling, and Ivan Tur-genev. And even Karl Marx, for the professor believed in examin-ing all points of view.

In the English class of another professor, Frank H. Fowler, Carl found what poetry could mean to him. Fowler introduced him to British and European literature. Carl was deeply moved by the work of Robert Browning, and memorized many of his poems. Writers like John Bunyan, Daniel Defoe, and Charles Lamb made him see how the capture of sounds and smells and sights, in sim-ple, direct language, could awaken your own senses.

Only a handful of American authors were included in those omnibus anthologies. British authors were valued more highly. American writers were little appreciated or encouraged. But one day Carl bought an old, used copy of Walt Whitman's *Leaves of Grass*, although it was not required reading. He would read it many, many times, discovering a poet who spoke directly to him, to everyman:

> I celebrate myself, and sing myself . . .
> For every atom belonging to me as good belongs to you . . .
> I loaf and invite my soul . . .
> I harbor for good or bad, I permit to speak at every hazard,
> Nature without check, with original energy.

And again:

> I speak the password primeval, I give the sign of democracy.
> By God! I will accept nothing which all cannot have their coun-terpart of on the same terms.

Gradually Whitman was taking his rightful place as the first poet of continental America and as the voice of democracy. The humanitarianism in *Leaves* and its progressive philosophy struck home with Carl. It was echoed in Populist thinking about what was wrong with American life and what might be done about it.

Compared to the series of photos taken as he entered college, this yearbook portrait shows a more serious, mature, focused Carl—a young man with a mission.

Professor Wright brought into class the writings of the Englishmen John Ruskin and William Morris. Ruskin, an art critic, attacked industrial society for treating the laborer like a machine, ignoring his soul and the soul's "right to see and enjoy the clear sky, works of art, health, sanity and beauty."

Morris—a poet, designer, and socialist—believed industrial mass production dehumanized both work and the worker. His utopian dream was of loving hand production where people would work not to survive but for the pleasure of craftsmanship. (How that would come about he left to the future.)

In an oratorical contest, Carl chose to prepare a speech about Ruskin. He crafted his language carefully, for impact on an audience's ear, for they would not see the words, and rehearsed it again and again. His passionate concern for what Ruskin, "A Man With Ideals," stood for, carried the audience, and he won first prize. It gave Carl greater confidence in his ability to write and speak out of the depth of his convictions.

Spokesmen for the poor and oppressed came to Galesburg, and Carl listened to their revelations of the underside of American life. There was Jacob Riis, the great reporter whose book, *How the Other Half Lives*, indicted slum conditions on New York's Lower

East Side, exposing them as "the evil offspring of public neglect and private greed." And Samuel Gompers, head of the cigar-makers union, who was now building a national labor movement with bread-and-butter goals. And there was Eugene Debs, the veteran union organizer and frequent socialist candidate for President.

To Carl, coming from a worker's family, their speeches made a great deal of sense. Industry had grown enormously by the 1890s. The rich were getting richer and piling up the means to invest and become even richer. The corporations their lawyers created dominated the oil, electrical, steel, and mining industries—and the railroads too, that August Sandburg labored for. But Carl could see that though plenty for all was becoming possible, there was still great inequality in American life. Corporate power not only controlled the workplace, it reached into the halls of government.

During those college years, exposure to great ideas and great writers led Carl to choose a writer's life for himself. In the books he read he probed for what made good writing good. How was it done? How did it make him feel sad or joyous? Angry or calm? What did writing do that reached into his heart? Strengthened his understanding? Under Professor Wright's guidance he learned to analyze writing, his own and others.

Of course he asked himself, could I do it? Would I be good enough? There was the fear of failing if he tried, but it didn't stop him. After all, if he didn't like what he wrote he could scrap it. (Which he would often do.)

Carl looked up a Lombard classmate who was now editor of a very small and obscure magazine, *The Thistle*, and submitted a poem to him. Late in 1902 "The Falling Leaves" reached print—his first published poem. Nothing else distinguished it, for it was trite, conventional.

He roamed New York, hunting for work, without luck. In his cheap hotel room he filled page after page of a pocket notebook. In it he copied out choice passages from books he was reading, lists of books he hoped to read, ideas for poems and lectures, phrases he heard on the streets, jokes, facts, statistics, words whose looks and sound he liked. Once it was expressive lines from Walt Whitman, describing cowboys: "Behavior lawless as snowflakes, words simple as grass."

To his sister, Carl wrote that he was passing through a sort of apprenticeship, in salesmanship and in dealing with people. "I'm a fool," he said, "but I know which way I am going." Did he? With his friend, Professor Wright, Carl exchanged poems by mail, and he sent some to Mary, too. After one long letter to his old teacher, Carl added, "I didn't know I knew that." (Which is what many writers discover when they find hitherto unexpressed thoughts and emotions flowing out of the pen.)

Underwood sent him to New Jersey to sell their slides. He spent only a few days a week at it, earning just enough to keep going. Meanwhile he was reading Shakespeare and Ibsen and Zola, and parts of the Bible over and over again. On the road he was losing his shyness, making new friends more easily than before.

In one New Jersey town he saw children working in the cotton mills under miserable conditions. Many as young as nine worked a twelve-hour shift, by night as well as day. Wages in the mills were so terribly low ($8 a week was tops) that families were forced to send their children to work. He found boys working in a glass factory for less than $3 a week. "They are grimy, wiry, scrawny, stunted specimens," he wrote, "and in cuss-words and salacious talk, they know all that grown men know."

The workers in such mill towns lived in wooden tenements jammed so close together that fires, vermin, and filth took a heavy toll on life and health. The death rate from malnutrition, exposure, and poor sanitary conditions was among the highest in the nation. Young children died at an appalling rate.

He was beginning to look at social injustice with the investigating eye of the great reporters of his time—Jacob Riis, Marie Van Vorst, John Spargo. He wrote about the exploited workers in an essay but also in free verse form, in a poem called "Mill Doors." In it he captured the grim reality of child labor:

YOU NEVER COME BACK
I say goodbye when I see you going in the doors,
The hopeless open doors that call and wait
And take you then for—how many cents a day?
How many cents for the sleepy eyes and fingers?
I say goodbye because I know they tap your wrists,
In the dark, in the silence, day by day.
And all the blood of you drop by drop
And you are old before you are young.
You never come back.

He was recording what he saw, in the light of what he felt. And he was learning how difficult it is to express your feelings with accuracy.

Carl met many young women while traveling the towns for Underwood—a schoolteacher, a banker's daughter, a church singer. "Delilahs," "Cleopatras," and "Salomes," he called them. They were attracted to his sturdiness, his good looks, his mellow voice, and the intensity of his feelings. He was dressing better now, taking on the look of the painters and poets whose pictures he studied. But in his mind he clung to the vision of The Ideal Woman who would come along some day and change his life.

At twenty-five, he was still earning only enough to barely get by. There were long gaps in his correspondence with his family. Unlike his sisters and brother, he didn't send money home. (He had none.) Nor did he go back to visit. Partly because he felt his father wouldn't welcome him unless he brought what he believed

freight bound west. But the railroad police caught him, and when

CARL THOUGHT HE MIGHT find the solution to security in Chicago. The big city—only thirty miles from Aurora—was within easy reach. Early in 1905 he began making frequent trips there, visiting magazine editors. He got to know the editor of a monthly journal, *To-Morrow*, a small magazine of freethinking opinion, who accepted some of his poems. One of these, "Petersburg," voiced Carl's enraged response to the event in January that triggered the failed 1905 revolution in Russia. When thousands of workers and students demonstrated in front of the czar's palace in the capital, his troops fired on them, killing hundreds and wounding hundreds more. The terrible news shocked the world. Using jagged rhythms and vivid language, Carl's poem marked a strong step forward in the mastering of free verse.

Although so different in temperament from his brother, Mart Sandburg understood Carl's needs and suggested he come home to take a job again at the fire station. It paid $75 a month, and would demand two hours a day of chores, plus action whenever the rare fires broke out.

Carl took the offer of a steady income and returned to Galesburg. He groomed the fire horses, exercised them, and cleaned their stalls. In between fires, he read, studied, and wrote in the corner of the upstairs room set aside for his use.

He read the socialist press as well as the daily papers, studied the Marxist classics, and continued to exchange poems with Professor Wright. Now and then he wrote pieces for the Galesburg paper, especially when he observed injustice being done—the abuse of tramps by police, or employers refusing to deal with unions. One of his columns lamented the frequent outbreak of wars around the world, and wondered why it was always the ordinary Joes—the workers, the farmers, the poor—who were drafted to do the fighting and the dying.

ART AND ARTISTS

When one of Carl Sandburg's younger sisters, Esther, wrote in 1907 to tell him of her enthusiasm for her piano studies, he replied with an encouraging letter that says much about his ideas on art and artists:

> What seems to me is necessary to make a success as an artist of any kind [is] this: Work and love, love and work. Live as your soul tells you you ought to live. Listen to what others have to say, good and bad, about what you ought to do and then do as your own soul, your own heart, your own self tells you. Thank God if you're not satisfied with your work. And don't worry. Go after big things. Tackle the delicate and subtle compositions, and tackle smashing and tremendous ones. If you don't play them to suit yourself or anyone else, you will have more power and skill just because you tried. Love the people you meet and do the best you can for them with all the heart and head you have, but don't allow anything big or anything petty, no combination of troubles of any sort to drag you away from your ambition or discourage you. Believe in yourself in the right way and then it will be easy enough to believe in others. Think yourself a piece of God's finest stuff and you will think better and do more for all others . . .

He liked this kind of journalism, and got more of it published than his poetry. He kept sending out poems and kept getting rejection slips. It didn't stop him from trying to do better. By now he recognized that free verse was his best, his natural form. His writing grew less awkward, less flowery, and became leaner and stronger.

He was at ease with his job and his writing, and enjoyed the renewal of affectionate ties with his family. But was life in Galesburg enough? After eight months, he decided to move on. He left that spring of 1906, never to live in Galesburg again. His mother understood his desire to change, but August still asked, "Is there any money in this poetry business?"

In Chicago, Carl dropped in on Harry Sercombe, the editor and publisher of *To-Morrow*. A wealthy man, Sercombe had made his large home both the editorial office and a center for poetry readings and public forums. If Carl would help with the magazine's editorial work, Sercombe would provide free room and board, but no salary. Carl stayed, moving upstairs in the center to live with several other young writers. It was a joy, he said, to taste this bohemian life. One young woman on the staff fell in love with him, but Carl wasn't ready for an enduring relationship.

The twice-weekly forums drew speakers like famous lawyer Clarence Darrow, British novelist H. G. Wells, settlement house pioneer Jane Addams, and Jack London and Edwin Markham, authors whose work Carl admired. It was a stimulating home to have— every day new people, new ideas, new tests of his own capacities.

Best of all, *To-Morrow* published both his prose and his poetry. The magazine let him write about almost anything he chose. This was the time when investigative journalists were commanding national attention for their exposés of what was glaringly wrong with business and politics. Although President Roosevelt thought that big business needed to be curbed, he feared the "muckrakers," as he called the writers, would spur the rise of radicalism.

Carl admired the detailed and careful studies of corruption in government and business. He believed writers had an obligation to speak openly on the issues of their time. He used the pages of *To-Morrow* to voice his own convictions. He attacked hypocrisy in religion and in politics, he argued against the death penalty, he fought against censorship and book banning. He followed up on Upton Sinclair's book, *The Jungle*, which exposed terrible conditions in the Chicago stockyards, with his own criticism of Swift and Armour, the giant meatpackers.

By 1906, only a few months out of Galesburg,
lecturer/orator/editor Sandburg has
many titles, but still virtually no income.

No mass audience was reached by what Carl had to say in that obscure journal. Yet it was the place where he learned to sharpen his observations, deepen his thought, and simplify his prose. Those who defended the status quo accused him of being unchristian, of being a radical. But those who read him with an open mind could see that at the heart of his writings was a love for humanity and a passionate desire to make life on earth peaceful and beautiful.

True, he did it without pussyfooting. He wanted, he wrote Professor Wright, "to play hell with fakes" and to "twist the tail of conventionality."

During that summer he began to feel the crowded life at Sercombe's was getting to be too much for him. The itch to move on seized him, and he retreated to a rented room in Aurora. He set up his old typewriter and tried to capture the teeming life of Chicago in new poems. Some he sent to *Reedy's Mirror*, a weekly magazine with a large national circulation. The editor rejected his work but gave him sensitive criticism. Right now you're more of a radical than a poet, he wrote Carl, but you can be both.

The editor was right. Both politics and poetry aroused Carl's passion, and he was radical in both. Though he still struggled with poems, he now put more time into public speaking. Maybe that would pay the rent. He heard every lecturer who came within reach, studying their techniques, gauging their effects upon the audience, crafting the development of his own themes. He tackled many topics: Whitman's life and work, child labor, the penal system, war, socialism. In one lecture, dealing with the "big theme" of the common man, he said:

> He is the essence of the tragedy of lost or mistaken opportunities. . . . He is the moving shadow of what might have been. . . . In a nation where poverty has put its finger-marks of shame on the door of ten million homes we may question whether there is "democracy" or "justice" or "liberty." . . . The Golden Rule cannot be evaded. To starve another is to starve yourself. We grow by acts of fellowship.

Bookings for his lectures were rare, and didn't pay much, either. He had to keep peddling the stereoscopic views, too. Giving up on freelancing, he took a job as assistant editor and advertising manager with *The Lyceumite*, a Chicago trade journal covering the lecture and entertainment circuits. For it he wrote biographical sketches of famous lecturers. With Chicago a great crossroads, he was able to hear many platform artists and to learn from them. Sunday mornings he went to a lecture series on evolution and

Incidentals, 1907, also published by
Professor Wright's Asgard Press, looked
more like a real book than Sandburg's
first effort, but again distribution was
limited and income virtually nonexistent.

socialism, and Sunday afternoons to public forums where anyone
could sound off from the floor on anything they liked: anarchism,
birth control, pacifism, single-tax, socialism, trade unionism. . . .

He filled notebooks with jottings for essays in what would be
his second book, *Incidentals*, to be published in 1907 by Professor

Wright's press. In April he lost his job when *The Lyceumite* merged with another publication. Back to selling Underwood slides on the road, barely earning the $4 weekly needed for room and board, he looked for lecture bookings but got only a few that summer. Once he reviewed his own performance (anonymously) in the local paper and praised it highly. (Walt Whitman had done the same. When his *Leaves of Grass* was published in 1855, he gave it a rave—unsigned—review in a Brooklyn newspaper.) Carl wasn't being false, for his thoughtful and passionate performances were being received with ovations. He respected the audiences, and would always give them his best. He despised lecturers who felt too superior to give their hearers more than a mediocre performance.

Back in Chicago as fall came on, he joined the staff of a new lyceum journal, for $20 a week. It gave him access to all the theaters and lecture halls, yet left him time to write more lectures—and to meet many young women. He wrote a friend that he had fallen in love and out again several times. These were only brief flurries of romance, and nothing came of them.

He lost his job within a month, but soon was offered another. This time he refused it. He was twenty-nine now, confident—even cocky—about his talents, sure that soon he would be recognized widely as an artist on the lecture platform.

My time has come, he told Professor Wright.

8

Politics and Romance

**N INVITATION** from a labor newspaper to speak to an audience of workers brought Carl to Manitowoc, Wisconsin, in October 1907. The editor drew readers by promising them a lecture on Walt Whitman that would surpass anything they'd ever heard before. The auditorium was packed that night, and the lecture was a triumph.

The editor let Carl write his own front-page review, not the first or last time Carl would be offered the chance to praise himself. "Sandburg," his unsigned review said, "proved himself a man of deep thinking ability and great oratorical power." Carl would reprint such praise in circulars promoting his lectures. He would even borrow a friend's name for attribution when he invented blurbs. "I am a ready liar in a good cause," he said.

The good cause was not just his own self-interest, but socialism. Many of the people in his audiences were socialists, at least in sympathy, if not party membership. The muckrakers had helped make the country take stock of where it was going. Their hundreds of articles and books, including Carl's own writings, reawakened conscience and started people thinking of what their duties were in the development of a free and democratic society.

On the lecture platform and at rallies, Carl dramatized the hard facts: Nearly 8 million women and about 2 million children were earning wages outside the home. Half the women averaged no more than $6 a week. Some 40 percent of the children held jobs where conditions were the worst and employers the most ruthless—in mines, factories, textile mills, tenement sweatshops. As for the men, three out of four earned under $15 a week. Hours ranged up to twelve a day, seven days a week. The industrial accident rate was shocking. Thousands were killed each year, and half those deaths were preventable. Hundreds of thousands more were injured every year.

In the face of such inequality, such suffering, some thought that reform was not enough. They worked for radical change in society. Eugene Debs, whose speeches Carl had gone to hear, questioned whether labor could ever gain anything real and lasting under capitalism. The economic system of private ownership of the means of production must go, he said.

Since the birth of the American Socialist party in 1901, socialist groups had struggled to find a following in America. By this time, socialists were publishing daily and weekly newspapers, had set up schools, and started their own book publishing houses.

The socialists tried to win labor's support, and made many converts within the unions. They put up candidates for local, state, and national office, too. In Manitowoc, where Carl had just spoken, both the mayor and the editor were socialists.

In Wisconsin the socialists were making gains in Milwaukee and other urban centers. Now they wanted to reach out to the rural areas. That November, Carl was appointed a district organizer for the party in the northeastern part of the state. It's not clear whether he asked for the job, or the party offered it to him. It seems odd, for Carl had no experience in political organizing, no notion of the administrative skills it required, and no record as a party member. What the Wisconsin leaders did recognize, however, was maybe more important—Carl's passionate concern for working people and their needs, and his great talent for speaking to their hearts.

But how to organize? They told him to hold meetings in halls or homes, speak on street corners to anyone who'll listen, build local branches where none exist, and galvanize action where they do exist. And if he did a good job, it would mean organizing day and night with little time for sleep. His pay? The dues he would collect, the money people would toss into the hat at public rallies, and the money paid when he sold the party's books and pamphlets.

So now I'm an "agitator," he wrote Professor Wright. And for what he called "constructive" socialism. No "pie in the sky" stuff. No, he wanted to organize people to fight for improvement in their own daily lives, right here and now. He didn't believe in sitting back and waiting for a socialist heaven to arrive "inevitably." He pointed to the reform measures socialist pressure had proved could be won in the Wisconsin state legislature.

He worked hard at his task, combing his district to recruit new members, recording in his notebooks actions planned and taken, dues paid, results won, prospects to be reached. He was getting down to the very roots of the socialist movement.

While he believed ardently in the need for change, Carl did not hold with those radicals who said it must be done "by any means necessary," including violence. Yes, the American promise of "life, liberty and the pursuit of happiness" had not yet been fulfilled. But its possibilities were alive, and American democracy provided the means to realize them. If only enough people could be mobilized to carry out reforms through the ballot box.

Soon after he began his work, Carl met Lilian Steichen at party headquarters. She was a beautiful woman of twenty-four (he was thirty), small in size, with lustrous blue-gray eyes, black hair, and a lovely voice. Her radiant personality captured Carl at once. She, too, was the daughter of immigrants, from Luxembourg. Her father was a copper miner and her mother a dressmaker. Her older brother Edward was a gifted photographer now living in Paris. Lilian, an honors graduate of the University of Chicago, was a high school teacher. She did volunteer work for the Socialist party. Carl asked her to have dinner with him that night. She already had a date, but she gave him her address. They parted, and soon began exchanging letters. It turned into a courtship by mail, for they shared the same intense feelings about politics and culture and romantic love. We'll always fight joyously for a better life for all, they told each other; we'll do "all the good we have strength to do."

The turning point was her discovery of Carl the poet. Although he wrote her that his days as a poet were over, he sent her a batch of his newer poems. She saw at once that his true calling was poetry. You're a wonder, she wrote, and called him "dear Poet-of-Our-World-Today." She was falling in love. Their letters grew more and more intimate and lyrical, though they had only

Lilian Steichen, sister of the photographer Edward Steichen,
fell in love with Carl's poetry and then Carl, himself.
She called him "Poet-of-Our-World-Today."

seen each other once. At last, in March, they managed to meet at her parents' home where they spent a week together. Edward Steichen, her brother, was visiting too, and he and Carl began a warm lifelong friendship.

Carl and Lilian planned to be married that summer. She was committing herself heart and soul to his writing, ready to fuse her life with his, ready to place the poet's needs above her own.

Back to organizing after their loving week together, Carl found farmers as well as factory workers ready to listen to socialist ideas. The party was growing nationally, and electing more and more people to office. Paula (Carl had given her the new name, preferring it to Lilian, and she accepted it) notified her school that she would resign at the time of her marriage. Each began to save for the start of a new household, hoping to have $50 by their wedding day.

They met again in Chicago in May, where Carl was a delegate to the national Socialist party convention, and they shared a hotel room for the weekend. The delegates were very diverse. They came from all parts of the country, representing some 3,000 socialist organizations, and many different occupations and ethnic groups. They argued fiercely in the debates over platform and candidate. But in the end they united in their choice of Eugene Debs as their presidential candidate. It was the third time he ran for the highest office.

Carl and Paula were married on June 15, in Milwaukee, at the home of a socialist minister. Carl's sisters Esther and Mary were there, and Paula's mother. They promised to love and honor each other—but not to obey. Afterward, they celebrated at her parents' farm. The neighbors gave them a shivaree—a raucous serenade with cowbells, horns, and tin cans. Carl capped the evening by taking up a collection for the Socialist party.

Paula stayed at her parents' farm and Carl returned to his party work. It was hard going, moving from town to town to rally the voters to support the Socialist candidates come election day in November. He also wrote a weekly column for the party's newspaper. Paula quickly saw that her expectation of sharing in his work would not mean doing it side by side every day. She was married, but there would still be lonely days, and weeks, and even months when they would be apart.

Their frequent letters helped bridge the separation and keep their love warm. Carl's organizing was so demanding that he had less time to feel lonely. He spoke in union halls, in factory yards, on street corners to groups of a dozen or crowds of hundreds. It was an intensive training in oratory, and through it he developed a magnetic style that would make him enormously popular on platforms and stages and in radio, TV, and recordings in the years ahead. Not that his speeches varied much. He relied on a few tested ones, but made every audience feel he was spontaneous and fresh, as though he were improvising every sentence. And like any fine actor, he reveled in the applause he earned.

One of his best contributions to the election campaign was his 5-cent pamphlet, *You and Your Job*. It documented in striking detail the key issues—child labor, the right to a job at decent wages—and argued for socialism as the remedy for the urgent needs of working people. The pamphlet was so effective that the party distributed it far beyond Wisconsin.

When the "Red Special," Debs's campaign train, crossed the country, Carl boarded it for the Wisconsin leg. He was deeply moved by this close connection with Debs and wrote Paula, "His face & voice are with me yet. A lover of humanity. Such a light as shines from him—and such a fire as burns in him—he is of a poet breed, hardened for war."

But the election results were terribly disappointing. The Socialists had been sure they'd win at least a million votes: They received less than half that. The Republican William Howard Taft easily beat the Democrat, Bryan, and Carl's candidate, Debs. Still, the Debs campaign had pressured both major parties into adopting some reform programs.

Now Carl and Paula set up housekeeping in Appleton, the heart of his district, in a rented three-room apartment. Taking stock of his prospects, Carl saw that all the hard work he was putting into politics would never support a family. As 1908 ended, he decided to give more time and energy to lectures than politics. It didn't lessen Paula's loneliness, for lecturing often took him away from home, to Michigan and Ohio, as he tried to earn decent money on the platform.

He distributed lecture circulars he composed himself, with tributes from people like Debs, who called him "one of the most brilliant young orators in the Socialist movement, a fearless exponent of the cause of truth and justice." Paula helped as his fulltime secretary, taking care of his correspondence and typing his writing. She praised him in her letters, trying to dispel his uncertainty, assuring him it would be all wrong to give up writing his great poems. "It's only a question of time till we come into our own." She believed in him more than he did himself.

That winter was harsh and stormy. With Carl still unable to make a living by organizing and lecturing, Paula tried to save money on food by eating only one meal a day, and on fuel by reading at night in the warm public library. Sharing the warmth close by were Appleton's homeless men and women. Paula's dream was to be able to buy a few acres somewhere and grow vegetables and raise chickens for subsistence. They clung to their political convictions but had to face reality. Carl now and then sent Paula poems written on the road. Bits and pieces were good, yet a long way from what would become his best work.

His prose was more vital and direct. In April, prospects picked up when *LaFollette's Weekly Magazine* began to publish Carl's "Dear Bill" letters, a series he was writing in the voice of an old villager, commenting on the life of these times. They proved so popular the editor would take all he could write, although able to pay only a little.

As an organizer, Carl often put in twelve-hour days, sometimes seven days a week, gathering only some $20 a month for his pay. The average wage of a worker was now $32 a month. And here were Carl and Paula, two highly educated and talented people, who gave themselves wholeheartedly to work, together earning less than the average underpaid worker. How much longer could this go on?

9

A Victory for Socialism

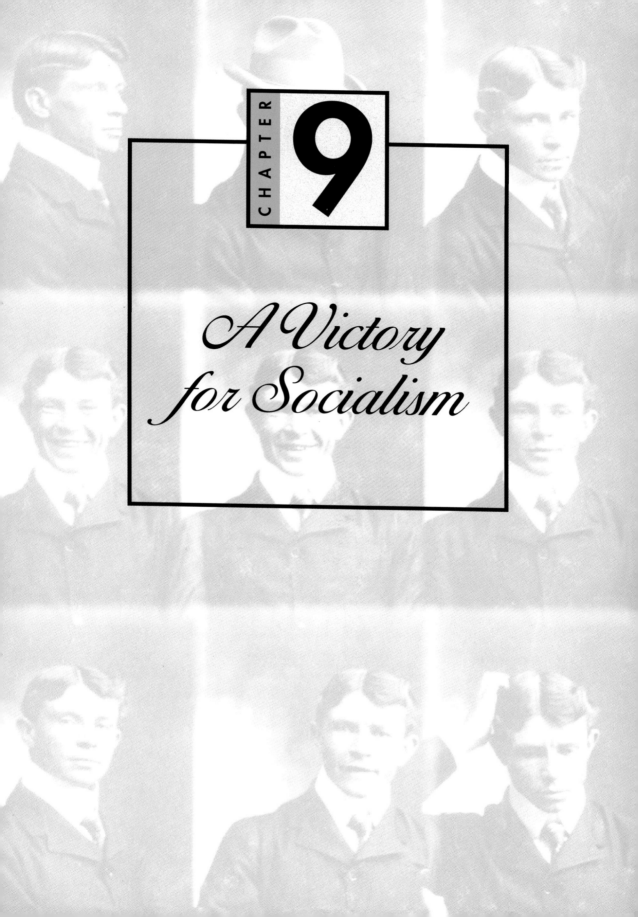

THE ANSWER WAS TO FIND A JOB—a job that would pay a living wage.

In June 1909, Carl went to Milwaukee, and was hired to write advertising copy for a department store. It wasn't his first choice. He had tried newspapers, but there was "nothing doing." One editor asked about his job history. Carl told him all, leaving out only that he had been a political organizer. "I didn't say what my politics are," he wrote Paula: "Am wondering what kind of liar I am." When the store took him on at $20 a week, even though he had no experience as a copywriter, Paula arrived to find rooms for them.

After six weeks of preparing ads to sell things to shoppers, Carl's conscience began to bother him. How could a socialist help capitalists to make profits?

That brief moral crisis ended when the *Milwaukee Journal* offered him a job. He was to write news stories and editorials, as well as a regular column. He liked the independence of the paper, and the chance to report on a vast variety of events and issues. While Paula welcomed a decent income, she pressed Carl not to forget his poetry. Although he was writing few poems, his work as a journalist fed him a rich supply of material that would eventually be reflected in his poems.

Tuberculosis was the big issue that Carl dug into that fall. A contagious and often fatal infection, TB was the cause of a national health crisis, taking 20,000 lives a year. Carl's articles put the spotlight on overcrowding and unsanitary conditions in many industries. Factory workers were the chief victims. Although TB had been a scourge since ancient times, there was still no drug treatment for it. All that doctors could do was recommend fresh air and sunlight, good food, and lots of rest. (Not until the 1940s would antibiotic therapy be developed.)

Caught up in the war on TB, Carl left the newspaper to join an anti-TB flying squadron. He gave lectures on prevention of the disease day after day as they traveled through forty-five cities in Wisconsin.

Then he and Paula pitched into the Socialist campaign to elect candidates for municipal offices. Emil Seidel, a German immigrant and craftsman, was the Socialists' choice for mayor of Milwaukee. While electioneering, the Sandburgs moved from a rented room to a plain little house in a suburb. Paula bought some chickens and started a poultry farm. Suddenly, news came that Carl's father had died. At sixty-five, retired from the railroad, August Sandburg had been working as a handyman in Galesburg. With voting day so close, Carl did not make the long and costly journey to attend the funeral. Many years later he wrote that his father had never wanted anything but to feed and house his family.

Pushing on tirelessly in the campaign, Carl's vivid oratory won the support of great numbers of working people. What had the old standby parties done for America, he would ask audiences. They give us only "Prosperity for the few and hell for the many. . . . We have learned that Labor will have to fight its own battles. From now on we trust OURSELVES." Paula, too, despite the hazards of raising chickens and the many sleepless nights it cost her, managed to help in the campaign by speaking to women's groups. She held up Abe Lincoln, the railsplitter, as an example of socialism's true spirit: "He would feel out of place anywhere except with the labor movement struggling for better food, better clothing and better housing."

Seidel won a resounding victory over the Republican and Democratic candidates. He swept into office with him a host of other local officials. It gave Milwaukee, a city of 400,000, the country's first socialist municipal government.

Like many American cities targeted by the muckrakers, Milwaukee was ridden by stinking slums, greedy landlords and banks and utilities, corrupt police, and corrupt courts. Carl was overjoyed by Seidel's victory. He would work his head off for this generous soul. They would fight for a practical program of improvements in everyday living—clean air and clean streets, more and better housing, a living wage, improved schools, vocational training, recreation for young and old.

Hearing of the socialist victory, Paula's brother Edward Steichen wrote them, "Wonderful to think that only a few years ago, a socialist was something common and base—sort of half-criminal. The world is a great place after all."

The first thing Mayor Seidel did was to appoint Carl as his private secretary, at $1,200 a year. The new socialist administration proclaimed a long agenda of reforms to create "a great city" with "the highest ideals of humanity." But socialists in office, Carl discovered, did not act like idealists in a dream society. On his job he had to deal with complaints, ambitions, selfishness, jockeying for power. Yet their administration did make some gains, even against constant attacks by a generally hostile press and the forces that stood to lose by honesty in government. Although Seidel would serve only one term, he set a pattern for decency in government that would be respected for many years to come.

That fall the job of city editor of the *Milwaukee Herald*, a socialist weekly, fell open. Carl quit the mayor's office, deciding that in this new post he could do more for his socialist ideals. A few months later, however, the party set up a daily paper to campaign in the coming elections of 1912. Carl became labor reporter and columnist for the *Milwaukee Leader*.

The nearly eighty pieces he wrote were solidly factual, direct, and clear. He had put behind him the soft, dreamy prose of earlier work. He also broadened his concerns, attacking the exploitation of women workers and of blacks. He freelanced articles, too, and even wrote more poems. Paula typed his work and sent it out. The prose usually sold, but few poems were accepted. Sometimes editors encouraged him to try them again.

The two major parties had learned from their defeat in the three-way election of 1910. This time they combined forces under a "Non-Partisan" banner. Seidel got three thousand more votes than in 1910, but the coalition defeated him. Carl wrote an editorial on the outcome. He said that if only the opponents of socialism realized that: "Back of all politics are the conditions of human life, the price of bread and meat, the hours that men stand on their feet and break their backs at productive toil, the terrible power of an employer to take away a man's job and thrust him suddenly into the street, the ever-present threat of a miserable old age without money or strength for work."

Again, for the fourth time, the Socialists' national convention chose Debs to run for president, with Emil Seidel as vice president. Sadly, by now, the once united socialists were split into warring factions: right wing, left wing, center. Bitter quarrels crippled the party's ability to function. The internal strife and tension were too much for Carl and Paula. With their first baby, Margaret, enlarging the family, and the need for calm and security, it seemed time to leave Milwaukee. Maybe they would make a better go of it in Chicago, the Windy City.

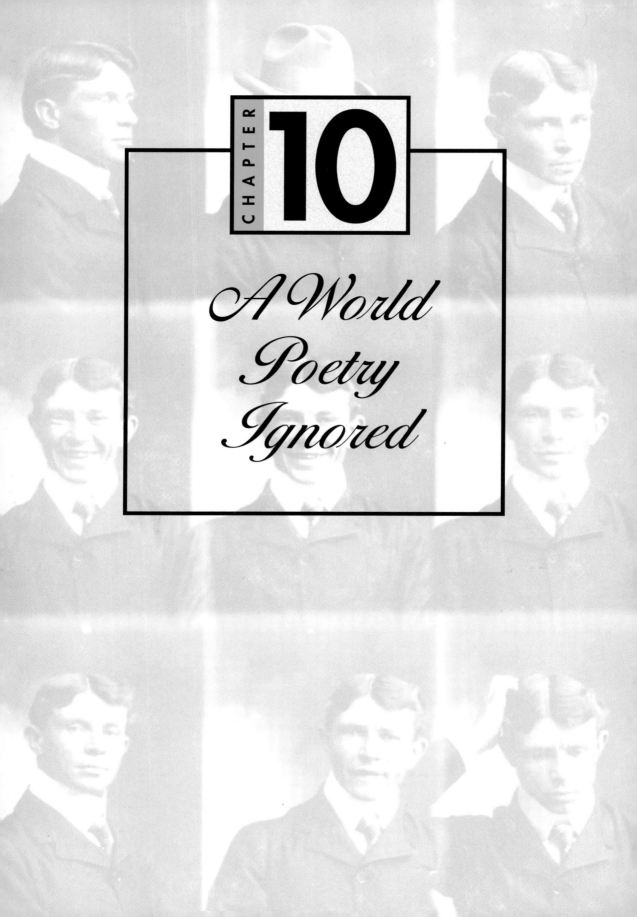

10

A World
Poetry
Ignored

**HICAGO PROVIDED NO EASY PATH** to security. Carl began at the *Evening World,* a socialist paper. He moved his family into a rented apartment in Ravenswood, a northeast neighborhood. Barely had they settled in when the paper collapsed. One newspaper after another turned Carl down. Desperate, he tried to get any kind of job, no matter what. It was one of the hardest times they would ever have— broke, no friends to borrow from, no prospects for work.

Early in 1912 his luck changed. *The Day Book,* a daily tabloid, took Carl on. The owner hoped to prove it was possible to reach working people with a paper that did not accept advertising but would be self-supporting at one cent a copy. The new job was doubly a good break for Carl. First, it paid $25 a week, and second, his editor, Negley Cochran, a political and social reformer, gave him the freedom to write about anything he chose. For the five years he would work there, he learned much of value from Cochran. In his reporting he got much closer to working-class life than ever before. And Cochran pushed his staff to write simply, sharply, sensitively, for the workers they wanted to reach.

At home Carl spent long hours every night on his prose and poetry. He wanted to shape an independent style to voice the tough issues that concerned him. One was the high rate of industrial accidents and how to avoid them. He offered two articles on it to *System: The Magazine of Business,* a large trade journal. The editor not only bought them, but asked him to come on staff as associate editor, for $35 a week. A ten-dollar raise meant a lot to a family man, and he switched jobs.

But again, it troubled his conscience as a socialist to be writing for a magazine whose aim was to show its readers how to make more money. Sometimes that feeling made him drop his own byline and use a pen name instead. Yet he could not resist giving his writing a pro-labor slant whenever possible. After six weeks of this, the editor got wise and told him he'd better leave.

Another job gone. Adding to the Sandburgs' misery was the loss of their second child, a baby girl who did not survive the birth. Desperate for work, Carl found a job at a small trade journal for the hardware business. It was hack writing that paid poorly, and again he used a pen name to sign his pieces.

At home he found an outlet for his pain and sense of failure in the poems he wrote. On his own, unaware of what other poets were trying to do, he delved into new subjects: the sights and sounds of Chicago, the workers in the factories, the shopgirls, the daredevils climbing into the clouds to build the new skyscrapers, the immigrants on the streets below, struggling to survive in a strange city of steel and stone. Permeating his work was the theme of loss, and the suffering it brought.

Carl wrote his poems in longhand and Paula typed them carefully. She sent them off to the magazines again and again. The rejection slips piled up. Carl knew his work was not conventional, and though disappointed, he was not surprised. The traditional stilted "poetic diction" was not for him. He had discovered in ordinary speech the strength of everyday life. He wanted his poetry to make a music that was more like the way people talked. Openly indebted to Whitman, Carl's poems were even more varied, more venturesome.

In an interview, Carl talked of his work habits: "I cut out all words ending in *ity* and *ness* as far as I can. That is, I cut out words describing 'state of being.' And I search for picture-words, as the Indians have them, as the Chinese have them."

He said writing poems wasn't easy. He spent a lot of time and energy—it could be a month or more—seeking just the right word. A poem of his might go through a dozen or more versions before he released it.

In the fall of 1913 Carl brought several of his poems to a small Chicago magazine called *Poetry: A Magazine of Verse.* It had only 1,500 subscribers, probably because it printed poetry of a new kind, that did not imitate what almost everyone else was writing. It was edited by Harriet Monroe, a native Chicagoan in her early fifties. She had traveled widely in America and Europe, and made

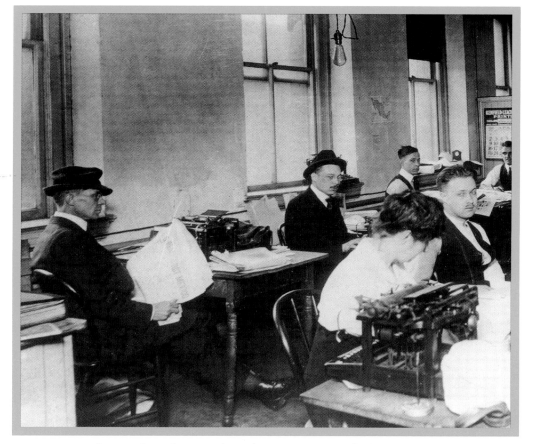

A photo of Carl at work in the newsroom of *The Day Book*,
a paper that "takes no advertising and therefore tells the truth."

many friends among artists and writers. Around 1910 she sensed
that a new era in American and British verse was about to open.
Herself a published poet, she raised funds from well-to-do friends
to assure the publication of the magazine for at least five years.

Her aim was to search out exciting new poets and new move-
ments, and to open the minds of readers to their work. She
believed poetry was ignored or neglected by the established cir-
cles of artists and critics. Her own passion for poetry led her to
serve creativity with economic support and honest criticism.

The *Poetry* office was in a decaying old mansion. Carl was greeted by Eunice Tietjens, a poet and assistant to the editor. Sandburg, she said, "was lanky, warm and human, slow-spoken and witty, his eyes very blue behind his thick glasses." His poems "took us all off our feet and it was with much pride that we introduced his new star to our firmament. . . . We adopted Carl at once and loved him. . . . He had a deep sympathetic sense of humor which always kept him from being the usual thumping radical."

His were "strange poems," said Monroe, "in very individual free verse, beginning with 'Chicago' as the 'hogbutcher of the world.'" Such lines shocked her at first, but in the March 1914 issue she gave Sandburg's nine poems the lead position. And paid him $70 for them.

By that time, Carl had left the hardware journal and gone back to *The Day Book*. Though his pay dropped, he would be much happier on a workingman's paper.

The Chicago poem reflected how Carl felt about the city. To a friend he wrote:

> You might say at first shot that this is the hell of a place for a poet but the truth is it is a good place for a poet to get his head knocked when he needs it. In fact, it is so good a place for a healthy man who wants to watch the biggest, most intense, brutal and complicated game in the world—the game by which the world gets fed and clothed—the method of control—the economics and waste . . .

Carl found that lots of people had their heads "all in a muddle about newfangled poetry." But Monroe didn't give up, though winning over the public was slow going.

Sandburg was not alone in what he was trying to do. Like the muckrakers, he turned a harsh eye on the shoddy materialism of American life. These writers' reports on the industrial turmoil, the rise of American empire, the slums of the great cities, and the growth of social consciousness influenced both his prose and his poetry. Carl said, "If I must characterize the element I am most often active with, I would say I am with all rebels everywhere all the time as against all people who are satisfied."

Rising young novelists of his day—such as Theodore Dreiser, Sinclair Lewis, and Sherwood Anderson—employed a penetrating realism. They criticized the success ideal, the ruthless quest for profit, the standardization of life.

In poetry, too, new forces were emerging. Poets had been frozen in a scholarly, genteel tradition—conventional themes, conventional forms. But now, men and women like Sandburg were testing a new freedom. They looked to those rare ones in the past—Walt Whitman and Emily Dickinson—who forged new forms and found fresh language. Writers like Vachel Lindsay and Edgar Lee Masters joined Sandburg in finding the common people as worthy subjects, and in creating for them a vision of the future.

Sandburg's rich imagination touched a world almost wholly ignored in poetry. He took on the daring task of humanizing the waste spaces in American life. He saw the power and potential of vastly increased productivity but also felt its cost in human suffering. At this stage of his life he was still hopeful; he believed that goodness and beauty would triumph over evil and squalor.

CHICAGO
Hog Butcher for the World,
Tool Maker, Stacker of Wheat,
Player with Railroads and the Nation's Freight Handler;
Stormy, husky, brawling,
City of the Big Shoulders:
They tell me you are wicked and I believe them, for I have seen your
     painted women under the gas lamps luring the farm boys.
And they tell me you are crooked and I answer: Yes, it is true I have
     seen the gunman kill and go free to kill again.
And they tell me you are brutal and my reply is: On the faces of
     women and children I have seen the marks of wanton hunger.
And having answered so I turn once more to those who sneer at this
     my city, and I give them back the sneer and say to them:
Come and show me another city with lifted head singing so proud to
     be alive and coarse and strong and cunning.
Flinging magnetic curses amid the toil of piling job on job, here is a
     tall bold slugger set vivid against the little soft cities;
Fierce as a dog with tongue lapping for action, cunning as a savage
     pitted against the wilderness,

Bareheaded,

Shoveling,

Wrecking,

Planning,

Building, breaking, rebuilding,

Under the smoke, dust all over his mouth, laughing with white teeth,

Under the terrible burden of destiny laughing as a young man laughs,

Laughing even as an ignorant fighter laughs who has never lost a battle,

Bragging and laughing that under his wrist is the pulse, and under his ribs the heart of the people,

Laughing!

Laughing the stormy, husky, brawling laughter of Youth, half-naked, sweating, proud to be Hog Butcher, Tool Maker, Stacker of Wheat, Player with Railroads and Freight Handler to the Nation.

A Cry
of the
Heart

WHEN HARRIET MONROE gave a banquet at the time she published Carl's *Chicago Poems*, he found himself in the presence of one of the world's great literary artists. It was the Irish poet and playwright William Butler Yeats. As the guest of honor, Yeats voiced Carl's own belief—that poets must express themselves "whatever that self may be." Cut everything artificial out of your language, he said, and develop "a style like speech, as simple as the simplest prose, like a cry of the heart."

To those who think writing in free verse is easy, Yeats said that it is much harder to write than rhymed verse. That night Vachel Lindsay read verse so much in the spirit of Carl's that they soon became close friends.

In his debut issue of *Poetry*, Carl was printed side-by-side with Yeats, Rabindranath Tagore of India (who had won the Nobel Prize for literature), Robert Frost, and Ezra Pound—new friends for him and Paula in this circle, as well as in the writers around *The Day Book*.

Monroe saw Carl as "a stalwart slow-stepping Swede" with "a massive frame and a face cut out of stone." She liked to listen to his "rich, low-pitched, quiet voice." Other friends included Theodore Dreiser, whose novel, *The Titan*, had just appeared, and Edgar Lee Masters, the poet whose *Spoon River Anthology* would astonish readers by its frank revelations of village life. They all shared a belief in the beauty of the fact.

In 1916, Carl hit his stride, as both poet and journalist. *The Day Book* had climbed rapidly to 14,000 readers, giving Carl a sizable audience. He usually wrote in prose, but now and then in verse. His poem "Fog" was inspired as he watched the fog over the harbor while on his way to interview a judge. While waiting for the interviewee to arrive, he wrote out some lines that were to later become famous.

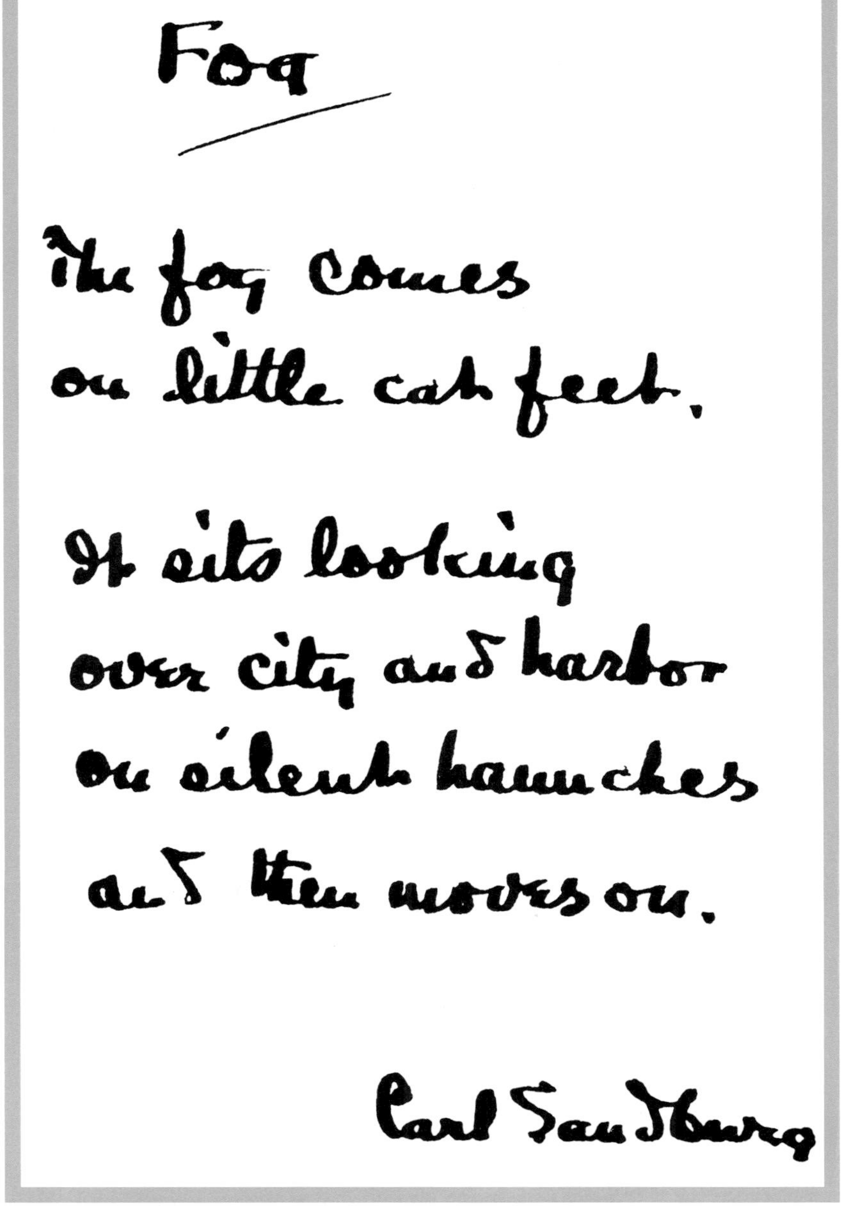

Fog

The fog comes
on little cat feet.

It sits looking
over city and harbor
on silent haunches
and then moves on.

Carl Sandburg

Sandburg's poem, "Fog," was written one day while
he was waiting to interview someone for *The Day Book*.
While waiting in the man's office, he jotted down
six lines of one of his best-known poems.

For several years Carl wrote pieces for the *International Socialist Review,* a Chicago monthly. Among the most striking were his articles on the report of the Commission on Industrial Relations. At the urging of President Woodrow Wilson, Congress had launched a three-year investigation of labor-management relations. The findings provided great details on the class conflicts Carl had seen for himself in his years of journalism. But the commission's report was technical, complex, full of jargon. Carl "translated" the report into simple, even blunt, language. This is how he wrote about the low wages employers were paying their workers:

> And say bo, how far do you think a working girl can go on $6 a week? It's way under the inside limits of a living wage. If she pays more than fifteen cents for a dinner, she's lifting nickels out of the money that ought to go for clothes. If she goes a little too far on clothes, she's taking nickels off her lunch money. Six dollars a week wages for one-half the wage-earning females of the United States is a fierce proposition when we look at the middle and upper class people who blow $6 for an opera seat, $6 for a week's automobile gasoline, $6 for a restaurant dinner for two, $6 for a pair of shoes or two pairs of gloves.

When the report brought up child labor, Carl wrote of "a big army of children of the working class worn to the bone. Thousands never learn to read or write their names. Hundreds of thousands are short-winded, played out, and no good when they grow up. And because the kids work, the father's wages have been cut."

The commission gave ample statistics on the huge percentage of national income swallowed up by the rich. Carl asked, did you know that "44 families pull down $1,000,000 or more? Most of these people don't work. They don't have to. The working class brings them everything they want and more than they can use."

He had little hope that laws would be written to correct social injustice. As Congress began a new session early in 1916, Carl wrote:

> Washington DC is the one place in these United States where they spill more bunk than anywhere else. Bunk? Take most any senator or congressman in the bunch of them and his first name

is Bunk. A few exceptions, yes. A few men with the nerve and the backbone to face real issues and tell the facts as they are. But mostly bunk shooters. . . . Less common sense, less ordinary human gumption displayed on the floor of the Senate and the House of Representatives and more hypocritical palavering than anywhere else on the map.

So he blasted away at those he saw as the enemy—the powerful few who ruled the workplace and the legislative chambers.

When a major strike of Chicago's clothing workers broke out in 1915, Carl reported it. He described police brutality against the picket lines, with photos to prove it, as well as pictures of pay envelopes with the wages marked on them: $2.66 for thirty-five hours of work, and $3.01 for forty hours. He was all for strikes and direct action to "force those capitalists to divide their profits, those withheld wages."

While he was writing daily reports on the clothing workers' fifteen-week strike, a book editor, Alfred Harcourt, wrote to say how much he admired Carl's work in *Poetry* magazine. He asked to see more poems; maybe a book would come out of it. With Paula's help Carl reviewed poems written over some fifteen years, and sent 260 of them to Harcourt. He called the collection *Chicago Poems.* Early in 1916 the book was accepted, and a few months later he tasted an author's joy in holding the first copy of a new book in his hands.

But some critics didn't welcome the book. Those stuck in the old formal ruts jeered at it. "Uncouth," "vulgar," "brutal," "coarse," a "violation of the English language," were just some of the nasty comments. Others, however, like the poet Louis Untermeyer, defended Carl:

> It cannot be said too often that he is brutal only when dealing with brutal things; that his "vulgarity" springs from an immense love of life, not from a merely decorative part of it; that his bitterest invectives are the result of a healthy disgust of shams; that behind the force of his projectile phrases, there burns the greater flame of his pity; that the strength of his hatred is exceeded only by the mystic challenge of his love.

One section of the book was called "War Poems." World War I had erupted in Europe in August 1914. It seemed nobody wanted the war, yet nobody could stop it. Old rivalries between nations had threatened the peace for many decades. A shot fired at Sarajevo, a remote Balkan town, set off a chain of explosions that shattered peace worldwide. As grim reports of mass slaughter seized the headlines, Carl, like many other poets, responded to the terrible news. His poem "Ready to Kill," contrasted the worker with the warrior: the first never honored for his constructive labor, the other idolized for killing:

> Ten minutes now I have been looking at this.
> I have gone by here before and wondered about it.
> This is a bronze memorial of a famous general
> Riding horseback with a flag and a sword and a revolver on him.
> I want to smash the whole thing into a pile of junk to be hauled away
>   to the scrap yard.
> I put it straight to you,
> After the farmer, the miner, the shop man, the factory hand, the fire-
>   man and the teamster,
> Have all been remembered with bronze memorials,
> Shaping them on the job of getting all of us
> Something to eat and something to wear,
> When they stack a few silhouettes
> Against the sky
> Here in the park,
> And show the real huskies that are doing the work of the world, and
>   feeding people instead of butchering them,
> Then maybe I will stand here
> And look easy at this general of the army holding a flag in the air,
> And riding like hell on horseback
> Ready to kill anybody that gets in his way,
> Ready to run the red blood and slush the bowels of men all over the
>   sweet new grass of the prairie.

Carl's antiwar poems appeared in several journals. He attacked the waste of war, the death of vast numbers of young men in battles ordered by a few old men, the suffering of mothers

The
INTERNATIONAL
SOCIALIST REVIEW

VOL. XV   JUNE, 1915   No. 12

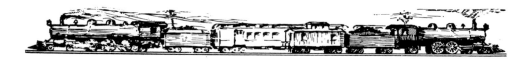

FIXING THE PAY OF RAILROAD MEN

By CARL SANDBURG

Third Article

RAILROAD firemen and engineers got beaten, soaked, trimmed to a finish, in the western railroad wage arbitration award handed down April 30. Because there were 65,000 of demands. That is, they got about one one-fortieth of what they asked for.

So ended the longest, the most expensive, the most thoroughly prepared and the most widely significant arbitration

Carl fought for social justice on many fronts and in many publications. Given his father's occupation, the plight of railroad workers was naturally one of his causes.

and fathers whose gift of life was being destroyed in the trenches. His images were violent, powerful, full of agonizing detail.

Carl kept writing articles, too, covering labor and politics. In 1915 the family had moved to a small house in Maywood, Illinois, buying it with a loan of $500 from a friend. Paula tended a vegetable garden in the backyard, and Carl had a study upstairs. In June another daughter, Janet, was born—a healthy, happy baby.

The war was the big issue in the 1916 presidential election. Wilson urged America to remain neutral and offered to help the nations restore peace. He was reelected. That year Carl and Paula left the Socialist party, though they would continue to support progressive causes. Perhaps he felt it better for himself as a poet and journalist not to be entangled in party politics.

Despite his call for neutrality, President Wilson soon began preparing for war. He broke diplomatic relations with Germany when it announced its submarines would sink any ship bound for Britain or France. On April 2, 1917, Wilson called on Congress to declare war against Germany. He demanded the enforced loyalty of all Americans in a cause that had split the country profoundly. "The world must be made safe for democracy," he said. The majority in Congress voted for war, and in we went.

Carl lost his job when *The Day Book* folded in July. He soon found another at the *Chicago Evening American.* Now he would be working for William Randolph Hearst, the publisher who had helped incite the Spanish American War Carl had served in. Only a year before he had accused Hearst of dabbling in treachery, invoking terrors of the unknown, using sex as a stage prop, and working on the elemental fears of the mob.

Perhaps the pay was irresistible—$100 a week to write editorials. And Hearst promised that he could say whatever he liked about anything. Things went well at first; he did write freely and was proud of those editorials. But when Hearst began insisting on *his* choice of subjects, and *his* point of view, Carl could stand it for only a few weeks. To stay meant selling out. The thought sickened him, and he quit.

He moved over to the *Chicago Daily News*, for half the sum Hearst had paid. It was an exciting place to work at a chaotic time in the nation's history. The *News* boasted several highly esteemed veteran journalists and a great editor, Henry Justin Smith. He put Carl to work writing editorials as well as reporting. Now that his own country was in it, what view should he take on the war he had attacked so powerfully in poetry and prose? He wrestled with crucial decisions everyone had to make.

Wilson approved emergency laws that gave the government the right to censor the press, ban publications from the mail, and imprison anyone who interfered with conscription or the enlist-

SMALL FOLLIES—GREAT DISASTERS

The cost of World War I, the first of a chain of international wars, was beyond calculation. Two million Germans, two million Russians, one million French, one million British, one million Austrians, and hundreds of thousands from other nations were shot, burned, bayoneted, gassed, bombed to death. Among them were the 30,000 American soldiers who died during the brief nineteen months America was in the war.

Long after, Freeman Dyson, a renowned scientist, said that it was "a war of peculiar ugliness, fought with exceptional stupidity and brutality . . . started for reasons that in retrospect seem almost trivial. . . . The First World War holds up a mirror to the present, showing how small follies lead to great disasters, how ordinarily intelligent people walk open-eyed into Hell."

ment of soldiers. His aim was to silence the antiwar opposition. If he could not have loyalty freely given, he would compel it.

The President helped spread the virus of fear. He attacked "hyphenated" Americans, accusing them of pouring "the poison of disloyalty unto the very arteries of our national life . . . Such creatures of passion, disloyalty and anarchy must be crushed out . . . The hand of our power must close over them at once."

That violent prejudice, mixed with a fear of radical ideas, sank deeper and deeper into the American mind. Before 1914, German-Americans had been highly praised as among our most worthy citizens. Now a mindless anger raged so high against them that people feared to speak German in any public place. Some state laws banned the teaching of German in the schools, banned German books from the libraries, forbade German or Austrian musicians to perform in public, and removed German composers from the performance repertory.

German-Americans suffered attacks on themselves and their property. A mob lynched a German-born citizen who had tried to enlist but had been rejected on medical grounds. "Patriotic murder," the defense counsel said, and the jury acquitted the mob's leaders. A labor organizer was lynched, and so was a coal miner—for refusing to buy a liberty bond. College professors were fired for daring to question the war. It was a whirlwind of hate and destruction.

The espionage and sedition laws invoked twenty-year sentences for any form of opposition to the war effort. More than a thousand Americans were indicted under them. The declaration of war tested the beliefs and the courage of American radicals. They had long opposed war waged for the profit of big business, and not for freedom and democracy. The American Socialist party split over the issue, the large majority voting against the war.

But now, from the hatred of war that fired his poems in 1914–1916, Carl shifted to support of the war. He had written patriotic anti-Kaiser pieces for *The Day Book*. And even as the government violated the free speech provisions of the First Amendment, Carl wrote that people shouldn't "embarrass the government in the conduct of the war." If their words or their actions gave comfort to the enemy, they should be "vigorously repressed" and harshly punished.

Yet other radicals stood bravely by their beliefs, even in the face of terrible persecution and punishment. Various pacifist and Christian groups spoke out strongly against the war, as did anarchists such as Emma Goldman.

What was the reasoning of prowar socialists? Carl expressed it in the *Daily News*: They could choose to be antiwar, suffer the consequences, and accomplish nothing. Or, they could choose to stand by passively. Or they could support the war, help to win it, and then build world socialism.

In the fall of 1917 Carl voiced his prowar position in a long patriotic poem called "The Four Brothers." It presented France, Russia, Britain, and America as "the four republics . . . sworn brothers to kill the Kaiser." It was published in *Poetry* and was an immediate success. Carl sent it to the government's central propaganda agency, which quickly distributed it to the press nation-wide and abroad.

Why did he change his mind? Maybe because he, too, shared in the patriotic love for America created in his and Paula's immigrant parents when they planted deep roots in their adopted country. He had served in an unjust war before, not questioning its nature. And perhaps when a German sub sank the *Lusitania*, a British passenger ship, with many American lives lost, it tipped the scales.

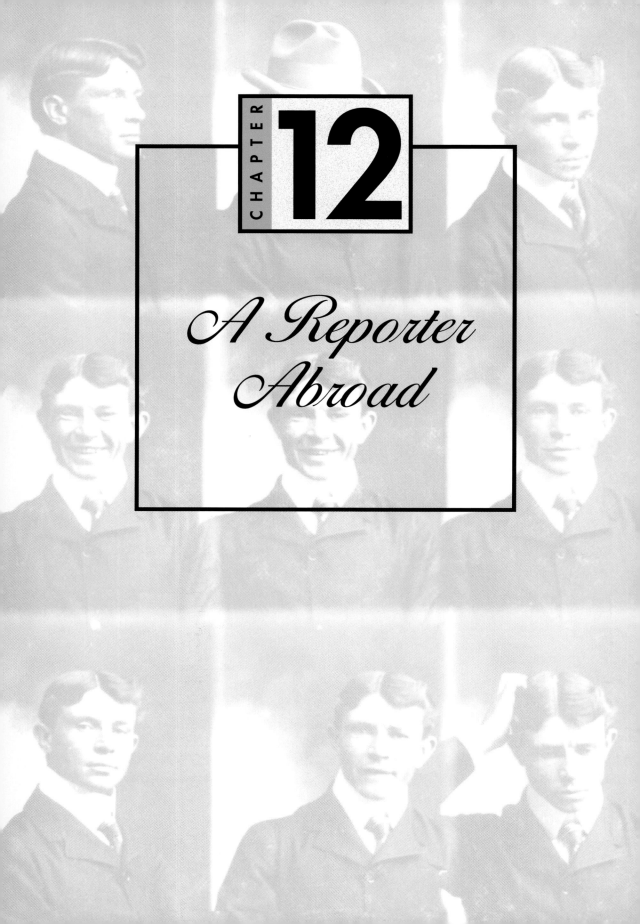

12

A Reporter Abroad

**ARL WAS ONE OF THOSE** rare people who could juggle several enterprises at once without losing any of them. By the spring of 1918, still deeply engaged in reporting, he offered Harcourt a second book of poems he called *Cornhuskers*. He told the editor it was "a bigger conceived and all round better worked-out book than *Chicago Poems* . . . a real and honest singing book." Harcourt agreed, and Harriet Monroe took the lead poem, "Prairie," for the July issue of *Poetry*. This time the prairie, not the city, was the book's setting.

With his manuscript on the way to publication, Carl tried to move closer to the heart of the war. At age forty he couldn't become a soldier. But could he go abroad to report the war? In July, the chief of the Newspaper Enterprise Association (NEA), a daily news service for over 300 papers, asked him to go to Stockholm as their correspondent for Eastern Europe. The Swedish capital was next door to both Germany and Russia, where the hottest news was being made. Carl said yes immediately. Half his salary of $100 a week was to be sent to Paula; the other half would be for him to live on.

It was hard for him and Paula to part. She was left with their two children and was pregnant with another. He reached New York where he expected to get his passport, but the State Department held it up. Meanwhile, he corrected proofs on *Cornhuskers* and made new friends among the artists and writers in Greenwich Village.

At last the passport came through, and by mid-October Carl was in Stockholm. The war would end in a few weeks. But another source of big news was the Russian Revolution. A revolt in February 1917 had overturned the czarist monarchy, and replaced it with a democratic, constitutional government. But in October of that year, the Communist (Bolshevik) party had seized power and was now engaged in a civil war with its opponents. Using every means possible, the Communists were seeking to impose a dictatorship over the Russian Empire.

Like any veteran reporter, Carl sought out people who could feed him news, gossip, rumors, tips, ideas. The reports he cabled to NEA revealed his sympathy with the revolutionaries in both Russia and Finland. But only a few of them were distributed by NEA, and these were severely edited. One of Carl's sources was Michael Borodin, who had been a Chicago teacher. He didn't tell Carl he was now an agent of Lenin's government. He fed Carl useful material to be added to the books, films, photos, pamphlets, and newspapers Carl picked up everywhere he could.

As the war ended, Carl felt all of Europe was "bordering on hysteria" with civil wars, terrorism, starvation, epidemics breaking out in many places at once. The brutal cost of the "Great War" to save the world for democracy made him sick at heart. He was lonely for Paula and home. Letters were very slow in arriving at both ends. On November 24, Paula had given birth to a baby girl, who would be named Helga. After only one month of reporting, Carl booked passage home for mid-December.

NEA cabled him that reliable news on Russia was very hard to get, and asked him to bring back everything he could to help the agency do objective reporting. Borodin, hearing Carl was soon leaving, gave him a mass of material. As a special favor, he also asked Carl to carry some money for Borodin's wife in Chicago, as well as $10,000 in bank drafts for the head of the Finnish Information Bureau in the United States.

It worried Carl to be carrying those bank drafts, and to forestall trouble he told the American consulate in Sweden about it. Suspecting that the Finnish man Carl was to hand the money to was one of Lenin's agents, like Borodin, the consul alerted the port officials in New York.

When Carl's ship docked in New York, government officials confiscated the materials in his trunks as well as the bank drafts. They grilled him for hours on end to see if he was a conscious tool of anti-American conspirators. Finally, early in January, he was given back some of his things, minus all the socialist or communist material. He returned home at last, to be greeted at the door by Paula with the new baby in her arms.

A month later, after difficult dickering with the government under the risk of indictment, Carl gave over control of all the material he'd brought in, and agreed that the United States could use it as it saw fit. He handed on to Borodin's wife in Chicago the money entrusted to him. But what happened to the $10,000 in bank drafts is a mystery.

Carl went to work for NEA in Cleveland for a short while. But he and Paula decided not to move there; they preferred Chicago. The NEA transferred him. He fed stories and ideas to the Cleveland office until May. Then the NEA chief fired him, even though he had told Carl he was a remarkable writer and a fine thinker. There was a hint that Carl's radical politics made them too nervous.

That feeling shaped some of the critical reviews Carl received for his book, *Cornhuskers.* Published in the fall of 1918, it lacked the support of the radical press for the simple reason that wartime censorship had killed that press. Generally, the reviews were mixed. One contrasted his two voices, the "ranting socialist" and the "pure poet." Another deplored the book as "half-cooked free verse," but recognized a few good moments. Some praised the short lyrics while lamenting the propagandistic longer poems. Robert Frost said, "Sandburg is better and better . . . a great find. He's man, woman and child all rolled in one heart." The book earned a half-share of the much desired annual prize of $500 for a volume of poetry given by the Poetry Society of America.

A month after losing his NEA job, Carl was rehired by the *Chicago Daily News*, as its labor and industrial reporter. (He would stay with the paper for thirteen years—his longest hold on any job.) That postwar year of 1919 shook the country from end to end with violent upheavals by labor. Many people had hoped the war's ending would bring a new social order of peace and plenty. But the war had fattened big business on great profits and made America the world's leading power.

Labor was determined to win its fair share of the bonanza. More than 4 million workers that year—one out of five—went on strike: 60,000 during a general strike in Seattle, 365,000 steelworkers in fifty cities in ten states, the police in Boston, and many others. The direct cause of labor's mass upheaval was the fact that the cost of living had doubled since 1914, while real wages were 14 percent less in 1919 than in 1914. Milk, butter, eggs, meat—all had shot way up in price. Boosting the strike wave was the open-shop policy of the industrialists, denying labor the right to organize and bargain collectively. They used the Red Scare as their main weapon, convincing millions of middle-class people that every strike was the beginning of revolution. The Red Scare rapidly became a tool in the hands of politicians and promoters to further their schemes. The historian Frederick Lewis Allen described its operation:

> Innumerable gentlemen now discovered that they could defeat whatever they wanted to defeat by tarring it conspicuously with the Bolshevist brush. Big-navy men, believers in compulsory military service, drys, anticigarette campaigners, anti-evolution Fundamentalists, defenders of the moral order, book censors, Jew-haters, Negro-haters, landlords, manufacturers, utility executives, upholders of every sort of cause, good, bad and indifferent, all wrapped themselves in Old Glory and the mantle of the Founding Fathers, and allied their opponents with Lenin. . . . A cloud of suspicion hung in the air, and intolerance became an American virtue.

No wonder, as his biographer Penelope Niven wrote, Sandburg "kept his silence on some national issues during the height of the Red Scare after World War I, shaken as he had been by the spy episode."

That summer Carl advised, "Look for struggle and more struggle and no stability at all for ten years."

13

Race
Riot

**ACK ON THE *DAILY NEWS*,** one of Carl's first assignments was to write a series of articles on the blacks of Chicago. The national press was reporting on outbreaks of racial violence in many parts of the country. Before 1919 would end, twenty-five race riots would ravage American cities. "The black worm" had turned, said one black editor. No longer would his people turn the left cheek when the right was struck. "For this awakening," he went on, "the color madness of the American white man alone is responsible."

Black troops had fought in Europe to make the world safe for democracy. Now, returning from the war, they found they had to fight for democracy at home. And they were as ready to die for it here as they had been in Europe. In 1919 there were eighty-three lynchings of blacks, several of black veterans in uniform, some of whom were burned alive.

Day after day Carl roved the black neighborhoods, talking to all kinds of people on the streets and in homes, factories, stores, barber shops, bars. How did they feel? What did they think? What did they fear? What did they hope for?

He helped readers understand that the tensions he observed had to be seen against the background of the Great Migration north of the blacks. When the war began in Europe in 1914, it cut off the vast tide of emigrants to America. Northern industries, straining to meet war orders, were short of unskilled workers. They sent agents south to recruit blacks, promising higher wages and better living conditions. Black newspapers like the *Chicago Defender*, circulating in the South, wrote of job openings up north, of friends doing well, and about the freedom and excitement of life in the big city. Come north, the *Defender* urged, where there is more humanity, some justice and fairness. Here you can vote, you can work, you can move about freely; your children can get an education.

Migration soared. A half-million black people moved north in 1917–1918 alone. Chicago's black population leaped from 40,000 to almost 110,000. Chicago, New York, and Philadelphia now had the three largest black communities in the country.

Blacks found jobs in iron and steel and auto plants, in the meat-packing and shipbuilding industries, and in railroad shops and yards. Much of the unskilled construction work and street mainte-nance was now being done by black people. Many took the domes-tic service jobs that the immigrants from Europe formerly held.

But many northern industries kept their gates closed to black workers. And in some places, as labor disputes broke out, employ-ers brought in blacks to break strikes. Ironically, that was the only way colored workers got their first chance at jobs in several heavy industries. Of course it drove black and white workers even farther apart, and made it all the harder for blacks to enter unions.

"Welcome" signs did not go up when blacks entered northern cities like Chicago. Most whites refused to live in the same neigh-borhoods with them. Housing construction had been kept down during the war years, and now two groups of workers—black and white—competed for scarce living space. Whites had been there long before. And when blacks tried to find homes in their neigh-borhoods, they took legal action to keep them out. If that failed, they often tried mob violence—or they just moved out. Swiftly whole neighborhoods became black.

In one Chicago neighborhood a big banner suddenly appeared, strung across the street. THEY SHALL NOT PASS! it read. A warning to new arrivals from the South: Stay out! When a black man moved a few blocks past that sign and settled in a home, a bomb tossed from a passing car wrecked it. It happened three times, and each time he rebuilt and stayed on, and other African Americans followed.

There were more than fifty such bombings in those bitterly contested Chicago neighborhoods. Ninety percent of the blacks settled on the south side. The whites took it as an "invasion," and banded together to keep blacks out. Tension increased as incom-ing blacks hunted desperately for a place to live, *any* place. Often what they found was nothing but a hole. The dreamed-of happier life had turned into crowded and filthy tenements overrun by rats, broken plumbing, and garbage-littered streets, disease and crime.

And all the while local, state, and federal government stood by and did nothing to resist discrimination and segregation, nothing to provide decent housing, good streets, or good schools.

Now work, too, was less plentiful as returning white soldiers took back jobs from those who had replaced them. The black people jammed into segregated neighborhoods grew even more restless, disappointed, and bitter.

The race problem, Carl wrote, is rooted in economic inequality. Back of all acts of discrimination, north or south, was the failure to give any colored man or woman a fair chance at a job. One of Carl's articles presented the platform of the National Association for the Advancement of Colored People (NAACP), which was founded in 1909 as the result of a recent race riot in Springfield, Illinois. The NAACP called for the vote for every black man and woman; an equal chance to acquire an education; the right to a fair trial and the right to sit on juries; defense against lynching; equal service on trains and other public carriers; equal rights to use parks, libraries, and other community services for which blacks, too, paid taxes; an equal chance for employment; and "the abolition of color-hyphenation and the substitution of 'straight Americanism.'"

On July 27, a black boy, enjoying a Sunday at the beach on Lake Michigan, swam past a rope and climbed up on a raft—an ordinary act, not worthy of notice. Except that the rope, by unspoken understanding, was there to keep white swimmers on one side and blacks on the other.

Whites ordered the boy off the raft, and some flung stones at him from the shore. Immediately black bathers nearby threw stones back. During the fight, the boy drowned.

In the preceding weeks, gangs of young whites had been roving Chicago's streets, trying to terrorize black people into staying out of some neighborhoods. Two blacks had been murdered.

Within a few hours of the drowning at the beach, wild rumors circulated throughout the city. Mobs began fighting in the streets. The terror lasted all night and into the next day. By Monday noon, twenty-four bodies were cold in the morgue. Hours later, as black people were on their way home from work, whites dragged them off streetcars and beat them. Instantly, blacks did the same to whites. The riot spread throughout the city. Many more on both sides were injured, and several more killed.

Black homes were raided and burned, and in retaliation white homes went up in flames. Over a thousand people, most of them black, were left homeless.

For thirteen days the city was a battleground over which 10,000 people fought. At the end, the casualty list showed 38 killed (23 blacks and 15 whites), and 537 injured (342 blacks and 178 whites, with 17 others unidentified as to color).

It was the worst race riot the country had ever known.

Carl's series—eighteen articles in all—was published as the first volume in a pamphlet library Harcourt Brace wanted to issue cheaply. The aim was to get across to a broad public the hard facts about troubling social questions. It was called *The Chicago Race Riots July 1919*. The pamphlet reached a wide audience and was praised for its balanced coverage of the race issue. It was reprinted fifty years later, in 1969, with a new preface by Ralph McGill, editor of the *Atlanta Constitution*. He said that what Sandburg wrote "indicts us as a people [still] addicted to folly and violent resistance to healthful social and political change."

In the fall of 1919 the Sandburgs moved from Maywood to Elmhurst, a suburb, with more space for the kids to play. They hired carpenters to expand and improve the house, and Paula planted a garden to surround it. After his daily work at the *News*, Carl would go upstairs to his new study to put together his third volume of poetry, *Smoke and Steel*.

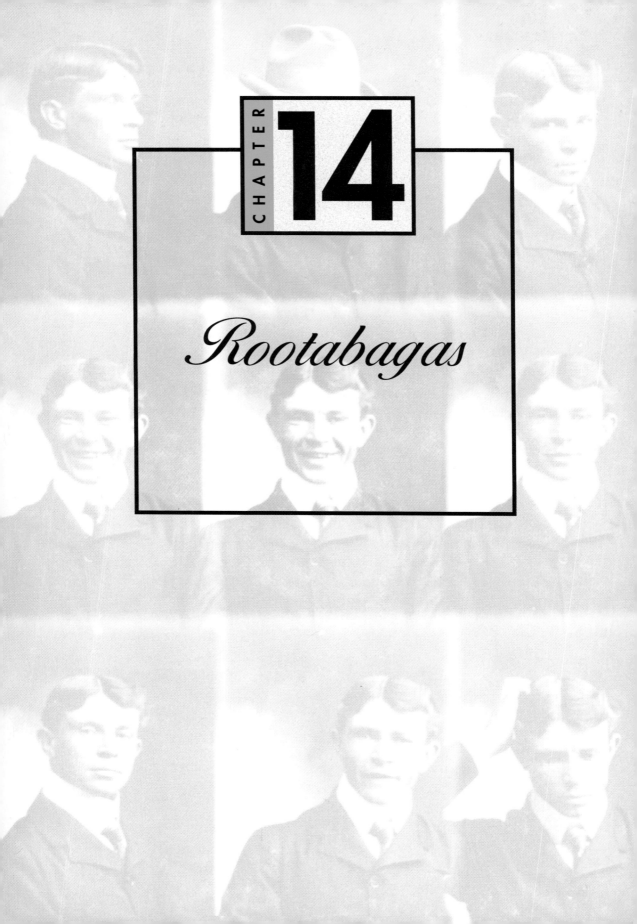

CHAPTER 14

Rootabagas

IT TOOK CARL MUCH OF 1919 and 1920 to prepare *Smoke and Steel* for publication. He revised old poems for it, and wrote new ones. The book reflected his love of nature, and the warmth of family life. Underlying several poems was his feeling of being alone in a strange world, of wondering who he was—a man of several identities? all unpredictably subject to change?

But he also continued to deal with the harsh life of working people, the blind craze of race riots, the greed of the rich. The ending of the war found Carl disillusioned with its outcome, with the way the victors divvied up the world. His poem "The Liars" runs headlong against his prowar poem, "The Four Brothers." He wrote "The Liars" in March 1919, five months after the war ended. It speaks of the leaders who lie to nations, who lie to the people, who meet behind locked doors to plot war and blow millions of people off the map so they can run the world and cash in again.

And if the liars invent another war? The poem predicts that the people will take things into their own hands next time—and refuse to fight. That bitter mood, registered so soon after the war, would be voiced again and again in the 1920s and 1930s in the memoirs and novels and poems of European and American war veterans.

Smoke and Steel, the title poem, is an epic of industrialism, as these lines from it suggest:

A bar of steel—it is only
Smoke at the heart of it, smoke and the blood of a man.
A runner of fire ran in it, ran out, ran somewhere else,
And left—smoke and the blood of a man
And the finished steel, chilled and blue.
So fire runs in, runs out, runs somewhere else again,
And the bar of steel is a gun, a wheel, a nail, a shovel,
A rudder under the sea, a steering-gear in the sky;

And always dark in the heart and through it,
Smoke and the blood of a man.
Pittsburg, Youngstown, Gary—they make their steel with men.

Often he sings of the creativity of workers. They *make* the steel, they *are* the steel. And in a shocking passage, he tells of an industrial accident, when steelworkers fell into a furnace of molten steel:

Their bones are kneaded into the bread of steel:
Their bones are knocked into coils and anvils
And the sucking plungers of sea-fighting turbines.
Look for them in the woven frame of a wireless station.
So ghosts hide in steel like heavy-armed men in mirrors.
Peepers, skulkers—they shadow-dance in laughing tombs.
They are always there and they never answer.

As Carl continued to work for the *News*, a friend wrote to him: "Give less time for journalism and more for creative work." Carl replied, "True, but I can earn a decent bricklayer wage the year round with newspaper work while three years sale of poetry would not keep my family six months."

Besides, his job fed rich human material into his poetry. *Smoke and Steel* grew from his coverage of the great steel strike of 1919. It was a crucial struggle to organize the unorganized in which twenty-two were killed, hundreds were wounded or beaten up, and thousands were jailed. Most of the steelworkers had been doing backbreaking labor for twelve hours a day at wages close to starvation level. Yet management ran press ads nationwide, smearing the strike as a communist plot to seize the steel industry.

After three-and-a-half months, the strike was lost. Said Senator Frank J. Walsh of Montana, it was because "the Government had taken sides with the employers."

Going to the picket lines and getting to know the workers made Carl their champion. His poems revealed their inner life, the pain and love and loss they shared. Their music, too—as he traveled the country, everywhere he went he collected folk songs, work songs, and spirituals. And jazz! He got to know many jazz musicians and captured their syncopated music in the poem "Jazz Fantasia." It begins:

Drum on your drums, batter on your banjoes,
sob on the long cool winding saxophones.
Go to it, O jazzmen.
Sling your knuckles on the bottoms of the happy
tin pans, let your trombones ooze, and go husha-
husha-hush with the slippery sand-paper.

Like jazz, the movies by this time had become one of America's most popular arts. In 1920 the *News* assigned Carl to write movie reviews. This was the era when film stars such as Charlie Chaplin, Douglas Fairbanks, Mary Pickford, and Harold Lloyd dominated the silent screen. Carl organized his work schedule so that he would see five or six movies over the weekend, and turn in his reviews by Monday night. That left him the rest of the week for his other writing.

As one of the first movie critics, Carl saw how powerful a medium film was in opening the world to audiences everywhere. Movies, he believed, could be a bridge between peoples. The motion-picture industry produced about 700 feature films a year, feeding them to eager audiences in 15,000 theaters across the nation and innumerable others abroad. Carl enjoyed thrilling stories, but he also favored movies that had ideas and challenged people to think. There were lots of them to challenge—20 million went to the movies each day.

He loved the originality of Charlie Chaplin's art, and felt "he spoke to all the people of the earth." On one of his trips to Hollywood to interview moviemakers, he visited Chaplin and then wrote a poem in tribute to his brilliant talents.

Like all performers, Carl himself heartily enjoyed the applause for his lectures. He turned more and more to public performances. They were unique—part recital of his poems, part singing of American folk tunes accompanied on his guitar, part "circus," as he described it.

EASY—OR HARD

You would think that a writer with Carl Sandburg's many achievements would find it easy to produce children's stories. No, he said, it's much harder to do than anything else. Writing the Rootabaga tales "is my refuge from the imbecility of a frightened world." But inventing zany characters risked going "a little too far out of the three dimension world for most people to get them." To let go with fantasy "takes a mood so different from the mood in which a man does his more factual work that the brain operates in two shifts like a day and night gang. . . . Fantasy, I suppose, must always be laid to one side, and 'tested' and 'tasted' in many ways, for a long time, before a fellow can be sure what are the good lasting high-spots. All that a fellow can do is to write his head off when the mood comes and the next day, or a week or two later, pick it up and look at it with the gravity of a lunacy commission."

At the age of forty-two, he had three young daughters. One of them, Margaret, had just been diagnosed with epilepsy, and soon another, Janet, as learning-disabled. He could not look to his poetry for support. The sales of poetry, with but few exceptions, had always been small. Some poets could afford to concentrate on their poetry; they had independent incomes, or high-paying professional careers, or had no family bills to meet.

So going on the lecture-recital circuit might be the answer to the family's needs. But there were other reasons, too, for shifting the focus of his career. The radical movement he had been part of for the past twenty years had been shattered. Many of its leaders were in prison. On January 2, 1920, ten thousand American workers, both aliens and citizens, had been hauled from their beds, dragged out of meetings, grabbed on the streets and from their homes, and thrown into prison by federal police under the direction of Attorney General Mitchell Palmer. The notorious Palmer raids, made simultaneously in seventy cities, resulted in many workers being deported. The raids were widely denounced as wholesale trampling on the people's rights. But they served their purpose. They frightened people and dampened their militancy, they weakened labor and helped keep wages down. The unions and the radical movement would not recover from the assault for another dozen years—not until the Roosevelt election would bring in the New Deal.

The Socialist leader who had earned Carl's affection and admiration, Eugene Debs, was in prison on a ten-year sentence for protesting the wartime sedition laws. Ralph Chaplin, a writer friend, wrote Carl from Leavenworth prison that eight radical prisoners had died of disease, seven had committed suicide, and five had been driven insane.

It's worth noting that Carl was the object of repeated government investigations. Herbert Mitgang (editor of the Sandburg *Letters*), in his book *Dangerous Dossiers,* records that in 1918, when Carl had that hassle with the government over the papers and money he had brought back from his Finland assignment, Army Intelligence began a file on him as a radical suspect. The FBI also maintained a file on Sandburg that would run to twenty-three pages. Mitgang says that "While many historians, poets and journalists offered words of praise for Sandburg's writings and statements, none could be found in his files." To the end of Carl's long life "the FBI was still tracking him and making entries in his 'C' for Communist dossier."

Such dossiers were a heritage of hysteria about radicalism. Sandburg was by no means the only writer policed by the federal government. The FBI also kept files on Pearl S. Buck, Robert Frost, William Faulkner, Ernest Hemingway, Sinclair Lewis, John Steinbeck, Robert Lowell, Tennessee Williams, Norman Mailer, Arthur Miller, and many more.

Even if Carl still wanted to write his searing indictments of the abuses of labor and of government complicity, where could he

Carl always found solace in coming home to his family.
From left, Helga, Janet, Carl, Paula, and Margaret

have published them? Then, too, the social criticism that had imbued his poems was dismissed as "old-fashioned." Art without politics was what critics looked for and praised.

Professor Philip Yannella of Temple University suggests that Carl "may simply have been written out—how many times could he have returned to the same themes, how many more poems could he have written about the working class?"

Parents love to tell bedtime stories to their children. Away from home so often as reporter or lecturer, Carl had all too little time for his three girls. But when he was with them, they enjoyed one another to the full. "The kids at home are a tantalization of loveliness," he wrote in a letter of 1920. "They are a loan, out of nowhere, back to nowhere, babbling, wild-flying."

As Margaret, Helga, and Janet begged for more stories, Carl looked for fairy tales that would please them. He loved the stories of Hans Christian Andersen—but where were *American* fairy tales? Where were stories with a native twist and zing and color? He began to make up his own tales, "tales with *American* fooling in them," he said.

His daughters, nicknamed "Sping," "Skabootch," and "Swipes"—loved them. Over the next ten years he created enough to publish three popular volumes of his *Rootabaga Stories*. In the dictionary the rutabaga is described as "a Swedish turnip with a large yellow root." (Carl spelled it his own way.) The tales are full of fantastic creatures, lovable and funny, yet human enough to echo our own folly and fantasy. As for the audience intended, he asked Harcourt to promote the Rootabagas "For People from 5 to 105 Years of Age." He meant, he said, "those grownups who keep something of the child-heart."

He began to read some of his Rootabaga tales when he performed on the lecture circuit. Invitations grew as his fame grew. By now Carl Sandburg was being called to every corner of the country. He had to space his lecture dates carefully, for his work at the *Daily News* came first. He was delighted to find "vastly different audiences" applauding him. With his Rootabagas he had ventured into a new field in storytelling. Those books would continue to sell long after his death, and not only in America but in translations abroad.

In 1922, Carl's fourth book of poems, *Slabs of the Sunburnt West*, was published, with Harcourt hailing Sandburg as perhaps "the most American of American poets." The book included a number of poems magazine editors had turned down as not equal to his other work. It led off with "The Windy City," a deeply felt poem about the birth of Chicago and its rise to a great industrial center. It hits at the "respectable" people, the upper-class snobs indifferent to the pulsing life of the working people and to the beauty of the city they created. The long title poem, which ends the book, was the only one about the Far West. It was his lyrical tribute to the Grand Canyon.

The book did not win wide critical approval. Many thought it was a mixture of his best and his worst. Carl's mother, however, took great pride in her son's work.

She wrote him, "I only stand bewildered and would praise God for having moulded his clay into a so beautiful piece of ornament in his kingdom."

Lincoln–
The Greatest
Poem

"**S**ANDBURG'S GREATEST POEM,**"** said a literary historian, is "his biography of Lincoln." Alfred Kazin, writing more than sixty years after the book appeared, went on to call it "a collective myth to the people, yes, who recognized the Civil War as one for their freedom. The book is a masterpiece because it weaves together thousands of American voices that finally established Lincoln as the awaited hero of a common people."

Nothing cost Carl so much time and energy as his life of Abraham Lincoln. When he first thought of doing it is not clear. But back on February 12, 1910, to mark Lincoln's birthday, he wrote a piece for Milwaukee's socialist newspaper. In it he presented Lincoln as a sort of socialist, a leader who would have detested the Republican party's use of him as their patron saint. To Carl, Lincoln was a guiding star for "the common people—the working class." Let's not forget, Carl wrote, that "Abraham Lincoln was a shabby, homely man who came from among those who live shabby and homely lives. . . . He never forgot the tragic, weary underworld from which he came—the world of labor, the daily lives of toil, deprivation and monotony. Against these things he fought. He struggled for more—more food and books and better conditions—for the workers."

A year later, again on Lincoln's anniversary, Carl wrote how ironic it was that Lincoln, a "loyal" member of the working class, was now honored by "grafters, crooks, political pretenders, and two-faced patriots who dine and fatten on the toil of workingmen." That adoption of Lincoln as his hero inspired fifteen years of research and writing.

Even as a boy, Carl was drawn to Lincoln. Born only fourteen years after Lincoln's death, Carl grew up knowing men who had known Lincoln, heard him talk, seen him off on the train from Springfield that carried him to the White House. In Carl's own Galesburg, 20,000 people had heard Lincoln debate Douglas on the crucial issue of slavery.

Without knowing what might come of it, Carl long ago had begun collecting anything and everything that had to do with Lincoln. By 1921 his files were bursting with material. When the Rootabaga book for children got off to a great start, Carl and Alfred Harcourt, his publisher, agreed that a biography of Lincoln for young readers would be a good bet. Especially if it focused on Lincoln's prairie boyhood, a time and place not so remote from Carl's own.

And so the work began, a labor of love that would create a masterpiece in six immense volumes.

The first necessity was to organize what he had already collected. He soon concluded that this would have to be a biography for everyone, not only for young people. He set about hunting for more material. He scanned newspaper and magazine files of Lincoln's time, dug out histories and biographies of the era, many long out of print, searched through both private and public collections on Lincoln. He worked at home, in his office at the *Daily News*, and in a rented studio in Chicago. Paula supported him in every way possible, diverting the children or visitors when he was deep in the work, helping with research, and taking a close look at his drafts.

When too many lecture dates were offered, he had to say no to some, favoring those that would bring him close to a Lincoln source. One date he would not fail to make was the invitation to the 1923 commencement at Lombard College, when Galesburg came out to see the local boy who made good receive an honorary doctorate of humane letters.

In October 1923, Carl sent Harcourt the first section of his Lincoln manuscript. He thought he could finish the book within another year. (It took far longer. The two-volume *Abraham Lincoln: The Prairie Years* would not see print until Lincoln's birthday in 1926.) Meanwhile, he had to juggle every possible source of income. His earnings in 1924—from the *News*, book royalties, and lectures—came to $4,752.89. Above average for that time, but scarcely enough to encourage lavish living.

Lincoln was already one of the most popular subjects for biography. Carl's approach was different, however—less political and more personal. He could not skim over the public actions, of course, but he wanted to dig more deeply than anyone else had to get at the mysterious, complex personality of the man—what he called the "silent workings" of Lincoln's inner life. Lincoln was fifty–two when elected president. How make the reader understand the years that had shaped him?

The biographer knows that the image he constructs is not reality itself. The reality is the ceaseless flux of that life, with its billions of moments of experience. That reality is the raw material from which the biographer works. Just think of the countless events in anyone's life that come one after another in the order of time. But Lincoln's own consciousness of those events was not Sandburg's. For Lincoln could not know, as Sandburg did, what lay in the future. And this is where imagination comes into play. Carl's mind had to be free to seek some arrangement or pattern in the life he was studying. In planning and writing his book he had to make connections, hold back some facts, foreshadow others, decide on juxtapositions, attempt to balance this element against that. He had to use documentary evidence in imaginative ways without departing from the truth. He had to give a form to flux, to impose a design upon chronology.

The portrait of Lincoln that Carl tried to create was a kind of collage, artfully putting together excerpts from letters, memoirs, anecdotes, news reports, speeches. Mixed in with what Lincoln said or did were the accounts of others who were witness to those words or actions. Carl had to judge the accuracy of these men and women from all walks of life—frontiersmen, farmers, laborers, lawyers, politicians, businessmen, family. Recall, too, how many different occupations Lincoln had between childhood and the White House. You can see how many facets there were to his development that Carl had to deal with.

Born in 1809 in a log cabin in the slave state of Kentucky, Lincoln came from a long line of pioneers who had inched their way west from the Atlantic coast. He was the son of an illiterate carpenter-farmer. His boyhood in the free state of Indiana was a ceaseless struggle against hardship and poverty. Add up all the days young Lincoln spent in school, and it comes to less than a year.

Then how did perhaps the greatest president we've ever had emerge from this beginning? Carl's treatment of Lincoln's coming of age surely was imbued with his memories of his own boyhood, for there were parallels. A biographer's writing is inevitably influenced by the author's own personality. Carl the poet was attracted to the most colorful details of Lincoln's life, to the emotionally inspiring. He selected what was most meaningful to him. It was not always what other biographers chose.

There were errors in *The Prairie Years* (most of them corrected in later editions) that critics pointed out. Not much space was given to interpretation. Carl flooded the reader with the facts as he saw them, expecting the reader to understand their significance in the light of the information given.

Although Carl's love for Lincoln is plain on almost every page, he did not picture a Lincoln with no faults. In a twenty-five-year legal career, Lincoln argued 6,000 cases. A shrewd lawyer representing both corporations and ordinary people, he used the tricky legal tactics typical of a profession out to win cases. In politics he was as practical and opportunistic as any candidate seeking office.

The finished manuscript ran to 1,000 pages, or 300,000 words. Dedicated "To August and Clara Sandburg, workers on the Illinois prairie," the biography came out in two volumes, at $10 for the set. Before the day of publication—on Lincoln's birthday—10,000 sets had been ordered. Harcourt knew it had a best seller. *Pictorial Review* bought the rights to serialize the book in five parts for $27,000, with $21,600 of it Carl's share. Hearing the great news while away from home, he wired Paula. "Fix the flivver and buy a wild Easter hat!" The family went off to Wisconsin on its first vacation ever.

It was Carl's biography that did much to create Lincoln as *the* American folk hero. When *The Prairie Years* was published in 1926, one reviewer found it "as full of facts as Jack Horner's pie was full of plums." Others said, "Here is God's plenty indeed," "a masterpiece which suits its subject" and "a veritable mine of human treasure from which to read aloud or to pore over for oneself." The

Just as Carl's biography did much to make Lincoln the
great American folk hero, so too did the publication of
Lincoln's story make Carl an American literary giant—and
a commercial success. He is shown here autographing
one of the volumes of the biography.

historian Allan Nevins, himself a noted biographer, commented
that Sandburg "was always primarily a poet . . . above all, a poet
with a strong sense of the values of democracy."

North Callahan, in his book about Sandburg, pointed out that
"Lincoln, like Sandburg, yearned for distinction. They both
courted the public favor in a way which could not be denied. They
both had an ambition possessed by few notable figures in all our
history, and each brought this ambition to fruition in an over-
whelming way."

CHAPTER 16

*They Sing
Because
They Must*

**HE SANDBURGS** would never again have to worry about money. In 1926, the year *Lincoln* came out, Carl's earnings were nearly $30,000. Feeling flush, they bought the summer house they had rented at Lake Michigan.

A year later, however, the Sandburgs decided to live permanently on Lake Michigan. The summer cottage was too small, so they bought land near Harbert with a splendid view of the lake and dunes. Paula designed a large three-story house with plenty of private space for their daughters, a big workroom for Carl on the top floor, and a fireproof storage space in the basement for his books and papers.

Carl continued to work at the *Daily News*, covering the sound films Hollywood had begun producing. It left him plenty of time to carry on his other interests. He began work on a new volume of poetry, and at the same time finished preparing *The American Songbag*—a collection of folk music he had been gathering ever since his hobo wanderings. It included 280 songs, more than 100 never before in print until Carl gathered them from railroad men, hoboes, convicts, cowboys, mountain people, work gangs, pioneer grandmothers—people who sing "because they must." Carl saw the music as a mirror of the nation's history.

Through these songs of the people he wanted to help Americanize the immigrants and their children. He had dug deep into the nation's history, its myths, its language, its music. Nothing could touch the soul of a people better than its songs. His book would demonstrate that history is not made up only of the acts of statesmen and soldiers.

Knowing only a few chords on the guitar, Carl got the help of trained musicians to prepare the settings for the songs. He would include not only the words and music, but also his notes on the history of the songs and how he had found them.

Just before 1926 ended, Carl's mother died, at seventy-six. She left a penciled message on a notepad—loving words about each of her children. Carl wrote a poem about her, although he never published it.

The burden of completing the *Songbag* was almost too much. Coming after the intense labor on the Lincoln biography, it caused a weariness he could scarcely bear. He was almost fifty now; it was hard to accept that he could no longer do all that he wanted. He was forced to rest, to sleep long hours, to diet. He turned down many, but not all, bids to lecture or write articles, explaining that his doctor had ordered him to be "a lazy bum."

Yet he took on a new chore at the *News*. In March 1927 he began a column called "Carl Sandburg's Notebook." Write about anything you like, said his editor. A few months later he neared collapse, so ill that Paula feared the worst. But as autumn came on, an enforced regime of no work and more play and more rest had him on his feet again.

He turned fifty in January 1928. The new house on the dunes proved a godsend. The walking, the swimming, the quiet hours restored his strength and his spirit.

The American Songbag (1927) was an immediate success. After it came what would be his last volume of poetry for many years. With *Good Morning, America* (1928) he began to speak less out of his own individual insights and more as the "Poet of the People." His originality was watered down. Critics rightly judged some of the poems to be trite and hollow. He failed to edit himself rigorously, and his editors at Harcourt failed him in this, too.

But that cannot be said of the ambitious title poem, one of the longest he ever wrote. It was a hymn of praise "to this great gorgeous shield of American earth," as one reviewer said. Its color, mood, and rhythm convey the joy of the spirit's renewal. If you hear it read aloud, you can't help but respond to Carl's tenderness, humor, and awe at the wondrous natural world.

The book is prefaced with Carl's attempt to get at the meaning of poetry. What is it? How does it work on us? He wrote thirty-eight definitions, using imagery of all sorts to explain what perhaps can't be explained. Read those thirty-eight; maybe you'll want to try your own definition.

Carl read the "Good Morning, America" poem on Phi Beta Kappa day at Harvard in June 1928, a sign that he had become a national celebrity. Everyone wanted him: Do this, do that, come here, go there, praise this, celebrate that. And of course, there were requests to write for all kinds of publications and occasions. Hearst, seeking to take advantage of the popularity of the Lincoln book, offered Carl $75,000 for a two-year contract to write a column for his chain of newspapers. It isn't clear whether he turned it down because he didn't like what Hearst stood for, or because he was no longer pressed for money. Maybe both.

He had begun work on the second and final part of the biography, to be called *Abraham Lincoln: The War Years*. He continued with the research methods developed for *The Prairie Years*, digging into Lincoln collections everywhere, combining lecture-recitals with research, absorbing what friends and specialists sent him. Some historians had challenged his use of sources in the earlier work, lamenting the lack of footnotes. This time he did his best to find the most reliable sources and to check them with authorities.

Once, talking to a *New York Times* reporter, he dropped a few hints about writing biography: "It would be a mistake to use any phrase that tended to draw the reader's mind back into the present," he said. Omit any references to situations or circumstances that come into being after the moment you are writing about.

He added he was glad he wrote about Lincoln's earlier years while still himself in his forties, for he was "closer then to the long, long dreams of youth." When he wrote *The War Years* he was in his fifties and sixties, and that was better, "because my judgment of men was better." He understood the older men around Lincoln as he could not have when he was younger himself.

The stock market crash in October 1929 triggered the Great Depression that would ravage the nation all through the 1930s. The Sandburgs were lucky to escape the worst effects. In 1929

Carl earned about $22,000—seven times the income of most working people.

At year's end, a large *Anthology of Revolutionary Poetry* appeared. "The world is tumbling about our ears," began the Introduction. The poems were drawn from writers worldwide, going back hundreds of years. For the Dedication, Carl's poem, "I Am the People, the Mob," was used, taken from his *Chicago Poems*, and four more of his poems were included in the book.

As 1929 ended, the noted film director D. W. Griffith offered Carl $10,000 to work with him for one week on a script for a movie about Lincoln. Carl said no, a good job couldn't be done that quickly, and proposed a $30,000 fee to cover more time. The deal didn't go through.

The economic crisis affected book publishing, like everything else. But Harcourt kept issuing whatever Carl wrote. In 1929–1930 there were two more volumes of Rootabaga stories, and *Early Moon*, a group of poems for children.

The Lincoln work moved more slowly than expected. It looks like a five-year stretch, Carl said. Still, on the side, he worked with a young Lincoln scholar, Paul Angle, on *Mary Lincoln: Wife and Widow*. Carl wrote the text while Angle prepared the source material and the notes.

In 1931, Carl lost his youngest sister, Martha, only thirty-nine, taken by illness. (Her husband, a railroad worker, had been killed on the job twelve years before.) That same year Carl's close friend, the poet Vachel Lindsay, ill for a long time and heavily burdened with debt, committed suicide.

In 1932, after three years of the Depression, one out of every four workers was jobless. The word "depression" seemed to have a permanent sound to it. A sense of hopelessness gripped the nation. America was a land of harsh contrasts. Surplus food was being dumped into the sea while men were breaking store windows to steal a loaf of bread. Shoe factories were shut down while children stayed home from school because they had nothing to put on their feet. Families went in ragged clothing while farmers could not market millions of bales of cotton. All this in the richest country on earth, with the fattest acres, the tallest buildings, the mightiest machines, the biggest factories.

As the presidential election of 1932 drew close, the Republicans renominated Herbert Hoover. They did it almost hopelessly, for he had found no way to halt the Depression. The Democrats chose Franklin D. Roosevelt, governor of New York, a man as hopeful as Hoover was discouraged. He promised experimentation and change, and in November carried all but six states, getting 22 million votes (including Carl's and Paula's) against Hoover's 15 million.

Carl's old party, the Socialists, for whom in the past he had worked so many years, got 900,000 votes. It was proportionately far less votes than in earlier times. Carl had once thought America had no choice before it but socialism or ruin. The election showed that most Americans didn't think that way. They were practical-minded: Deal with a problem when it comes up. If it doesn't work, try something else. Few, like Carl himself now, believed in a single solution that would solve all problems. No such answer was possible, and in all likelihood it would do more harm than good.

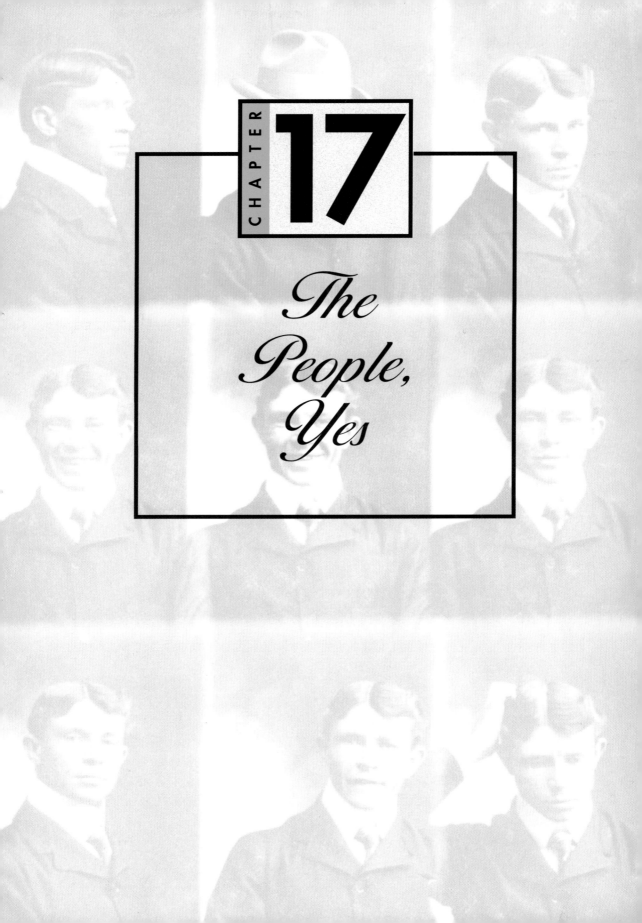

CHAPTER

17

The People, Yes

IS PHYSICAL AND MENTAL powers restored, at fifty-one Carl was able to be even more productive than before. Although he escaped the economic hardships of the 1930s, he was never indifferent to the troubles of others, and helped those in need. As a youngster he had seen his own family and community hit badly by the hard times of the 1890s. When FDR took office in 1933, Carl saw parallels between Lincoln's struggle to meet the great issue of slavery and FDR's to end the economic crisis. He thought the President and other government officials might learn much from that earlier history.

In 1935 he wrote Roosevelt that he was the "best light of democracy that has occupied the White House since Lincoln. . . . All the time you keep growing. . . . The People have done something to you and made you what you could not have been without them." Later FDR took Carl on a personal tour of the rooms and objects in the White House intimately connected to Lincoln.

In 1933, Carl was elected to the National Institute of Arts and Letters, despite the protests of conservative members who could not stand his kind of radical poetry. But the Depression years were reviving the spirit of the working class literature Carl had created decades earlier. As one critic said, who writes better proletarian poetry than Carl Sandburg?

While in the thick of work on *The War Years*, Carl began to respond in poetry to the devastation of the Depression. He wanted to reaffirm his faith in the "plain people." He would call it *The People, Yes*. It was a long poem, and grew longer almost by the day. Late in 1935 he sent the 112-page manuscript to Harcourt. This poem, he said, "holds some of the chaos and turmoil of our time and of all time."

Like his early poems, the new book was intensely critical of "the masters of finance and industry." They failed to realize that everything they had was sweated out of the people who did the work. Never, he told a friend, had he seen "greed, fear, brutality

His career peaking, and his health excellent,
Carl enjoys a peaceful moment with Paula, 1934.

among the masses to surpass what may be seen among the rich." He always had stood "with the people as against the exploiters of the people." He feared that unless the people Roosevelt called the "economic royalists" showed some concern for human needs, something terrible might happen. Yet he was not rigid about his ideas. "I have been wrong often in my life," he said, adding that he knew there were "many kinds of fools" inside himself.

Long before, when Carl was in his early twenties, he jotted down in his notebooks jokes and sayings and slang and mottoes and proverbs and legends and characters he picked up along the way. He had never stopped doing that, and much of it was poured into the epic poem. He called it a memorandum of the people, his record of what he had seen and heard of life in America. Like Tom Paine, he was a propagandist for democracy, a pamphleteer in poetry, trying to bring together "the people of the earth and the family of man," as Lincoln had once said. The poem speaks of the hardships of the Depression as well as the enduring strength of a people with a long history of struggle for human dignity, a decent living standard, and democratic rights.

Some readers wondered, is this really poetry? Even the most negative critics saw that if some of it was not, a lot of it was. In it was both prose and free verse in Carl's own rhythms and with his own intensity. What the 1930s had moved Carl to say echoed what he had said before, again and again. The people always have been the creators, the makers, the doers. Out of their ranks have come the great ones the world remembers. Always, too, the people are exploited, cheated, robbed of their just due. Sometimes they rise in revolt. But too soon they forget the wrongs done them and sink back into apathy. They will find salvation only when they figure out their ultimate destiny and move toward a better future.

But what that destiny is, and how to realize it, he never answers or explains. Although it came in the midst of the Great Depression, the book-length poem struck a note of optimism. The people—with all their limitations and drawbacks and handicaps—but THE PEOPLE, YES!—they would find their way.

The book was the climax of a long career as a poet—his sixth and final volume. Its greatest distinction is his use of the language of the people as his voice. He was at home in their lingo as no other poet before him had been.

The People, Yes was published in 1936, on the eve of FDR's election to a second term in the White House. By this time New Deal legislation had guaranteed labor the right to organize. The Congress of Industrial Organizations (CIO) was leading the struggle of the miners and auto workers to win union contracts. The dramatic sitdown strikes they initiated resulted in great gains for labor. When news came that the corporations had yielded to union demands, Carl was moved to the point of tears. He could not but remember what his father had endured those long years in the railroad foundry, wearing his life out for the pennies tossed him.

The writing of *The War Years* consumed him. He did most of the work at his old typewriter in the attic room. In good weather he moved out to his sundeck. When the pace tired him, he renewed himself with a long walk along the shore or a swim in the lake. The whole family pitched in to help with the small but essential chores so immense a project demands, but not always happily, for sometimes his daughters would have preferred the beach to the workroom.

He read and assessed what everyone else had written about Lincoln. But what meant most to him were Lincoln's own words— the speeches, letters, notes, memos, legal papers. Carl recognized that Lincoln was one of the great masters of the English language, with a gift for writing that placed him far above his contemporaries. Carl ranked Lincoln not only as our greatest president but the greatest writer among our presidents. His genius with words was recognized by the foremost writers of his own time—Walt Whitman, Ralph Waldo Emerson, Nathaniel Hawthorne. Carl's aim was to capture the power and the lyrical quality of Lincoln's feeling about democracy and freedom and equality.

Carl learned that no issue of the Civil War that confronted Lincoln was ever easily solved. The events of those stormy, bloody years were so twisted and tangled that it took infinite patience and resolve on Carl's part to make sense of them for himself. And to convey that hard-won understanding to his readers.

By the summer of 1938 the end was in sight. The manuscript totaled a million and a quarter words. While he tried to be as direct and open as possible, he knew that some readers—many perhaps—would have trouble making their way through the immense web of details. He believed he had done his best—revising, cutting, reorganizing—but it was time to call a halt. His last task was to collect the photographs required to illustrate the biography.

When Harcourt read the manuscript of 3,400 typed pages, he decided to publish it in four volumes, as a boxed set, priced at $20. And convinced he had a magnificent book to offer the public, he ordered a first printing of 20,000 sets. Soon additional thousands had to be ordered.

Reviews of the book were carried prominently everywhere. Carl's portrait landed on the cover of *Time* magazine. Critics called the biography "monumental" and "the greatest of all Lincoln biographies." The old college dropout won the Pulitzer Prize in history in 1940 and shuttled from one campus to another to receive honorary degrees.

Years later, in 1954, Carl completed work on a one-volume edition of the Lincoln. He cut huge swatches out of the original six volumes, and added a preface and some new material and insights. He knew many people would never have the time to read the immense original work, nor the money to buy it. With the one-volume edition, he hoped to bring his beloved Lincoln to still more readers.

So What Am I?

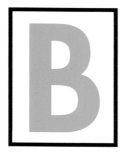**Y 1939—THE YEAR** Carl's final volumes on Lincoln came out—war clouds gathering over Europe were visible in far-off America. Carl was painfully aware of Adolf Hitler's rise to power in Germany and feared his regime could destroy peace in the world.

At the end of the year Carl wrote Thomas Mann, the great German novelist now in exile in America, that "Should any regime similar to the one prevailing in Germany now by any fate attain power in this country I do not doubt my choice would have to be that of death or exile."

Carl had watched foreign conflicts multiply during the 1930s: Mussolini's Fascist Italy invading Ethiopia, Japan invading China, Franco's Fascist troops overthrowing the democratic government of Spain. He had written many poems about wars and the cost they laid upon the people. He knew of "the secret arrests and the public atrocities and the studied punishments of concentration camps." But, he asked, "What do the people get for the wars they fight with each other?" In 1940 he went to a reunion of the men he had served with in the Spanish-American War of 1898. What had that achieved but to launch America on empire-building?

That same year he joined Dorothy Parker and Helen Keller to help the American Rescue Ship Mission transport Spanish refugees from France to Mexico to save them from seizure by Hitler and Franco.

As Hitler's tanks rolled over Poland, a great many Americans believed the United States should stay out of war at all costs. Descend into the storm cellar, they said, and let the hurricane blow over us. The desire to isolate America from the clash of arms was so strong that Roosevelt could not get Congress to adopt even a modest program of collective security. The legislators feared such measures might drag the country into war.

But as Hitler began to overrun Western as well as Eastern Europe, a change of heart took place. FDR and the Congress took one step after another to make America "the arsenal of democracy." Huge amounts of money and energy were pumped into speeding up American military production. Jobs were once again plentiful in a country just emerging from the longest economic depression in its history.

On the night before the 1940 election, Carl gave a five-minute radio talk to an estimated 80 million listeners. He called on them to reelect FDR. Like Lincoln facing the Civil War, he said, Roosevelt would be the best choice "in this hour of national fate."

Letters poured in asking for copies of the speech. And once again Carl plunged into political action. He wrote both poetry and prose to gain support for the antiFascist cause in the war. In 1941, a musical setting of *The People, Yes* was broadcast over CBS Radio. He began to write a weekly column for the *Chicago Times* syndicate, voicing his views on national and international development for the next two years.

In spite of the isolationists, the Roosevelt administration gradually edged its way into the war. FDR presented the struggle against Hitler as a righteous cause, and early in 1941 held up a vision of a new world order to be founded upon the Four Freedoms—freedom of speech and expression, freedom of worship, freedom from want, and freedom from fear.

On Sunday morning, December 7, Japanese naval forces launched a devastating attack on the U.S. naval base at Pearl Harbor in Hawaii. The next day the Congress with only one dissenting vote, declared war on Japan. Three days later, Germany and Italy supported their Axis partner, Japan, by declaring war on the United States.

If any war could be called a "just" war, this seemed to many, including Carl Sandburg, to be it. Few were spoiling for a fight, but after Pearl Harbor 96 percent showed in a poll that they considered World War II a necessity. What else could you do against a brutal power like Hitler's but resist it?

Carl gave advice to government officials on the best ways to win public support for the war effort. He wrote soundtrack narrations for government films, spoke at national unity rallies, printed patriotic poems, wrote the text for a photography exhibit, "Road to Victory," shown here and abroad. Yes, he was helping to provide propaganda for the war, but didn't writers have a responsibility to speak to their times? The enemy was always trying to win public opinion to its side. It was his job to speak for the side he believed in with all his heart.

In 1943, Harcourt published *Home Front Memo*, a selection of Carl's newspaper columns, poems, and speeches on the war. People kept urging him to run for Congress, and FDR told him he'd welcome such a liberal supporter. But no, said Carl, he was a writer, not a politician. Then MGM, the movie studio, asked him to write a novel based on a producer's outline for an epic film about the United States. They offered him $100,000 for nine months' work. He was sixty-five now, and had never tried his hand at a novel. It intrigued him, and in 1944 he began writing it. It took not nine months, but over four years. Published in 1948 as *Remembrance Rock*, it was over a thousand pages long. Although the public liked it, the critics didn't. They called it an artistic failure and said that he failed to create living characters or to sustain so long and sweeping a narrative.

The book was never made into a film. The war was long over by the time he finished it, and MGM had other interests to follow. But the novel itself simply wasn't good material for the screen. Later, in the early 1960s, another film company, 20th-Century-Fox, would pay Carl $125,000 to contribute his ideas for another epic film, *The Greatest Story Ever Told*. It was about the life of Jesus.

Soon after the war's end, the Sandburgs moved their home from Michigan to North Carolina. Carl bought a 245-acre farm in Flat Rock. Their three adult daughters and two grandchildren moved with them. Helga, their youngest daughter, now twenty-seven, was divorced and the mother of two children.

The prime reason for moving was the desire for a more temperate climate. Winters in Michigan were hard for the women to take; they had stayed put in that harsh season while Carl often escaped to warmer regions. And they all wanted more rooms, greater privacy, and space to expand farming. They found the right place close by Hendersonville, North Carolina. Their estate,

The Sandburgs were to spend many happy years in their
Flat Rock, North Carolina, home, which they named
Connemara because its setting resembled that region in Ireland.

which they called Connemara, embraced mountain, meadow, and forest. The three-story house, standing on the crest of a hill, had been built in the 1830s. The estate was named Connemara because its setting resembled that region in Ireland.

Moving from the Midwest to the South severely taxed Carl's strength. He was sixty-seven in 1945, in the midst of the novel, and playing with other projects in his mind. Over the years he had accumulated vast stores of manuscripts and letters and files and books and newspapers. The job of examining it all and selecting what to move and how to dispose of the rest was dismaying. But with the family's help it was finally done. It took a whole railroad boxcar to transport the seven tons of cargo from the old to the new home. Settled in at last, a friend heard Carl say, "What a hell of a baronial estate for an old Socialist like me!"

Here amid the Blue Ridge Mountains, Paula continued her work raising her ever-larger herd of championship goats. The goats provided lots of milk, butter, and cheese, and the family garden produced all the vegetables they needed. The daughters helped with the farming. Paula's specialized skills had already earned great recognition. She published articles in the journals in her field, made speeches, and won international awards for her breed of goats.

The 1950s were full of bad news, both personal and political. The spread of communism in Europe and Asia in the years following the war was seen by the United States as a threat to national security. To ferret out radicals and dissenters in government ranks, President Truman launched a federal loyalty investigation and many states followed suit. "An old Socialist" like Carl had seen persecution of radicals long ago, and here it was again. The wave of suspicion among Americans was played upon by unscrupulous politicians like the young first-term Senator Joseph McCarthy of Wisconsin. No one was above suspicion to this self-appointed witch hunter. It was shocking to see that the state where Carl had once organized for a socialist commonwealth was now identified with McCarthyism. An old friend, editor of a Wisconsin newspaper, spoke out against McCarthy and asked Carl to protest publicly. But he remained strangely silent.

People used to believe that peace, not war, was the normal state of affairs. Now they were told that the world was fated to be always preparing for war against the Communist menace. The first big war came in Korea in 1950–1953. Carl no longer felt up to commenting on events by writing newspaper columns. But who could ignore the sizable military campaigns or paramilitary CIA operations in former colonial or dependent countries on an average of every 18 months—Iran, Guatemala, Indonesia, Lebanon, Laos, Cuba, the Congo, British Guiana, Dominican Republic, Nicaragua.

And, of course, the big one: Vietnam. It was the century's longest and most controversial war, starting well before the United

States got into it. The nine years of U.S. involvement began in the 1960s, and the war would still be going on well after Carl's death.

It was hard enough to watch the killing fields proliferate all over the globe. At Carl's age, what brought death all the closer was the departure of beloved family and friends. One after another, they died on him. Old age was also a time in life, however, when recognition might arrive for one's achievements.

In 1951, Carl won the Pulitzer Prize for poetry with the publication of *The Complete Poems*. Recall that it was his second Pulitzer, for in 1940 the Lincoln biography had earned the first one. So what am I, he asked, poet? biographer? historian? troubadour? fairytale teller? The reviews of the huge volume—a life's work— were generally good, which surprised Carl. Yes, he knew maybe a fifth of what he wrote was dated and should be read with an awareness of how time changes things. Sometimes he was just "running off at the mouth," as he himself said. But after all, he did write that stuff, and let it go into print, so now he'd better shut up about it.

In the early 1950s Carl searched his memory of childhood to write *Always the Young Strangers*. It is the autobiography of his first twenty years. Published when he turned seventy-five, in 1953, it is rich in detailed sketches of family, pals, school, work, adventures. Few books offer so vivid a picture of midwestern life in the last decades of the nineteenth century. Called by the press "a triumph," and "the best autobiography of an American," it was welcomed abroad, too, as a universal story of coming of age. On almost every page you feel Carl's love of people and of country. He is not blind to evil, but it does not corrupt him. He is not driven by ambition. He seeks only goodness, to find it and to create it.

For the next several years Carl tried now and then to carry his childhood memoir forward. But the manuscript was never finished. After his death it was edited and published in 1983 as *Ever the Winds of Chance*. His biographer Penelope Niven speculates that what may have delayed completion of his autobiography was the McCarthyite atmosphere of the 1950s that trashed the socialist dream he had striven so many years to realize.

Public honors continued to descend upon him in the last years of his life. Schools were named for him, birthday celebrations were

The Sandburgs in 1953 at Carl's seventy-fifth
birthday party, celebrated along with the
publication of *Always the Young Strangers*.

organized in several cities, he read his work over the radio and on
the new medium of television, and was interviewed by the press
and on the popular talk shows. Both Ernest Hemingway and
William Faulkner, the novelists, when each was awarded the Nobel
Prize in literature, said the award ought to go to Carl Sandburg.

One of the projects Carl was proudest of matured in 1955, when
the Museum of Modern Art in New York opened an immense pho-
tographic exhibit drawing upon images worldwide of *The Family of
Man*. It was designed and organized by Carl's brother-in-law,
Edward Steichen, who asked Carl to write the Prologue for it. The
exhibit and the book based on it expressed their common vision of

the oneness of the world. In Steichen's words, they hoped to make people see "what a wonderful thing life was, how marvelous people were, and above all, how alike people are in all parts of the world."

It was Carl who called Steichen's attention to a phrase of Lincoln's, "the family of man." Within a few years more than nine million people had seen the exhibit in some seventy countries. And in book form, *The Family of Man* became the most successful photography title in history, selling way over five million copies.

On February 12, 1959, Carl was asked to address a Joint Session of Congress to mark the 150th anniversary of Lincoln's birth. He wove Lincoln's words into a portrait of the man and his times and their significance for the America of today. He kept giving lectures, singing, playing the guitar, appearing on major TV shows, giving endorsements and testimonials, collecting fees to enlarge the estate he would leave his family.

In his last years, Carl was not able to put in the long hours of work at home or on the road that he had been accustomed to. His mind still generated new projects, but his memory and his energy would fail him.

A dinner was held in New York to mark Carl's eighty-fifth birthday, with many notables in the world of literature and the arts attending. Moved by their warm tributes, Carl said only that "being a poet is a damn dangerous business. Here and there you are good, and here and there you are not."

In his last few years he lived quietly at Connemara, rarely leaving home. He read and reread his favorite old books, walked in the fields, slept a lot. His last trip was made in the fall of 1964 when he traveled to Washington to receive the Presidential Medal of Freedom from President Lyndon Johnson at the White House.

Perhaps the recognition that mattered to him most came when the National Association for the Advancement of Colored People made him a lifetime member, praising him as "a major prophet of Civil Rights in our time." He had "found beauty in brotherhood," the NAACP said.

It seems likely it was Alzheimer's disease that finally took Carl Sandburg down. On July 22, 1967, he died. He was eighty-nine. The last word he spoke was "Paula."

ALL MY LIFE

Carl Sandburg concluded his preface to the *Complete Poems* with these words:

> I am still studying verbs and the mystery of how they connect nouns. I am more suspicious of adjectives than at any other time in all my born days. I have forgotten the meaning of twenty or thirty of my poems written thirty or forty years ago. I still favor several simple poems published long ago which continue to have an appeal for simple people. I have written by different methods and in a wide miscellany of moods and have seldom been afraid to travel in lands and seas where I met fresh scenes and new songs. All my life I have been trying to learn to read, to see and hear, and to write. At sixty-five I began my first novel, and the five years lacking a month I took to finish it, I was still traveling, still a seeker. I should like to think that as I go on writing there will be sentences truly alive, with verbs quivering, with nouns giving color and echoes. It could be, in the grace of God, I shall live to be eighty-nine, as did Hokusai, and speaking my farewell to earthly scenes I might paraphrase: "If God had let me live five years longer I should have been a writer."

The news of his death went quickly around the world. The *New York Times* wrote that he was "more than a poet, biographer, spinner of tales and wandering minstrel—he was the American bard." His ashes were buried at his birthplace in Galesburg, Illinois. Ten years later, Paula died, at ninety-four. Her ashes were placed beside his.

POSTSCRIPT

I REMEMBER READING Carl Sandburg's poems when I was in high school. My English teacher said here is something new and different. We had been reading Keats and Browning and Poe and Longfellow. I enjoyed their music but was not deeply moved by it. This was the time when the Great Depression of the 1930s was ravaging America. My own working-class family—like millions of others—was having great trouble making a go of it. One day I came across Shakespeare's little poem, "To the Poor":

> Famine is in thy cheeks.
> Need and oppression stareth in thine eyes,
> Upon thy back hangs ragged misery;
> The world is not thy friend; nor the world's laws.
> The world affords no law to make thee rich;
> Then be not poor, but break it.

Different though the language was, the reality captured in those six lines struck hard. They were written more than 300 years ago. Yet they voiced my feelings now. And then the teacher read some of Sandburg's work to us. It was from his *Chicago Poems*. The quiet, lovely "Fog," of course, and then, knowing what joblessness had done to our families, his "Muckers"—

> Twenty men stand watching the muckers.
> Stabbing the sides of the ditch

133

Where clay gleams yellow,
Driving the blades of their shovels
Deeper and deeper for the new gas mains,
Wiping sweat off their faces
With red bandanas.
The muckers work on . . . pausing . . . to pull
Their boots out of suckholes where they slosh.
Of the twenty looking on
Ten murmur, "Oh, it's a hell of a job,"
Ten others, "Jesus, I wish I had the job."

Long after, when I was writing a biography of the poet Langston Hughes, I learned that he, too, had a teacher who opened the way to Sandburg's poems. Sandburg sang of the steel-towns and the workers they ground down, just what Cleveland's steel mill had done to Langston's stepfather. So moved was the young Langston by Sandburg's poetry that he wrote about it for the school paper:

Carl Sandburg's poems
Fall on the white pages of his books
Like blood-clots of song
From the wounds of humanity.
I know a lover of life sings
When Carl Sandburg sings.
I know a lover of all the living
Sings then.

Nearing his eightieth birthday, Carl was asked, "What do you want out of life?" He grinned, let loose with a laugh that began deep down, and said:

"All my life I've been thinking about What do I want out of Life? Mainly five things: first of all, to be out of jail. Second, to eat regular. Third, to get what I write printed. And next, let's say a little love at home, a little nice affection hither and yon, over the American landscape. And then, maybe the fifth thing I need. It seems like every day when I'm at all in health, I got to sing."

A NOTE ON SOURCES

THERE IS AN IMMENSE AMOUNT of material available to anyone interested in Carl Sandburg's life and work. His own writings first of all: his poetry, his autobiographies, his life of Lincoln, his letters, his books for young readers, and some ten volumes of miscellaneous writings.

More than a dozen authors have published their studies of Sandburg. Of all of these, I found Penelope Niven's biography the most valuable for its rich detail. New light on Sandburg's early professional life comes from Philip Yanella's portrait of the radical Sandburg before he won fame as a hero of popular culture. Yanella lists and analyzes nearly 200 articles by Sandburg unearthed from the archives of left-wing newspapers and magazines. Many of these I was able to examine at the Tamiment labor and socialist collection in the Bobst Library of New York University.

But nothing will serve you better than to read Sandburg himself.

SELECTED BIBLIOGRAPHY

POETRY

In Reckless Ecstacy. (as Charles A. Sandburg) Galesburg: Asgard Press, 1904.

The Plaint of a Rose. (as Charles A. Sandburg) Galesburg: Asgard Press, 1904.

Incidentals. (as Charles A. Sandburg) Galesburg: Asgard Press, 1907.

Joseffy. (as Charles A. Sandburg) Galesburg: Asgard Press, 1910.

Chicago Poems. New York: Henry Holt, 1916.

Cornhuskers. New York: Henry Holt, 1918.

Smoke and Steel. New York: Harcourt, Brace, 1920.

Slabs of the Sunburnt West. New York: Harcourt, Brace, 1922.

Selected Poems. Ed. Rebecca West. New York: Harcourt, Brace, 1926.

The People, Yes. New York: Harcourt, Brace, 1936.

The Sandburg Range. New York: Harcourt, Brace, 1957.

Harvest Poems. New York: Harcourt, Brace, 1960.

Honey and Salt. New York: Harcourt, Brace, 1963.

The Complete Poems of Carl Sandburg. New York: Harcourt, Brace Jovanovich, 1970.

Breathing Tokens. Ed. Margaret Sandburg. New York: Harcourt, Brace, 1978.

Billy Sunday and Other Poems. Ed. George and Willene Hendrick. San Diego: Harcourt, Brace, 1993.

BIOGRAPHY

Abraham Lincoln: The Prairie Years, 2 vols. New York: Harcourt, Brace, 1926.

Mary Lincoln: Wife and Widow, with Paul Angle. New York: Harcourt, Brace, 1932.

Abraham Lincoln: The War Years, 4 vols. New York: Harcourt, Brace, 1939.
Abraham Lincoln: The Prairie Years and the War Years, 1 vol. New York: Harcourt, Brace and World, 1954.

AUTOBIOGRAPHY
Always the Young Strangers. New York: Harcourt, Brace, 1953.
Prairie Town Boy. New York: Harcourt, Brace, 1955.
Ever the Winds of Chance. Eds. Margaret Sandburg and George Hendrick. Urbana: University of Illinois Press, 1983.

LETTERS
The Letters of Carl Sandburg. Ed. Herbert Mitgang. New York: Harcourt, Brace and World, 1968.
Carl Sandburg, Philip Green Wright and the Asgard Press. Ed. Clifton Waller, Barrett Library. Charlottesville: University of Virginia Press, 1975.
The Poet and the Dream Girl: The Love Letters of Lilian Steichen and Carl Sandburg. Ed. Margaret Sandburg. Urbana: University of Illinois Press, 1987.

MISCELLANEOUS WORKS
The American Songbag. New York: Harcourt, Brace, 1927.
Steichen the Photographer. New York: Harcourt, Brace, 1929.
Early Moon. New York: Harcourt, Brace, 1930.
Storm Over the Land: A Profile of the Civil War Taken Mainly from Abraham Lincoln: The War Years. New York: Harcourt, Brace, 1942.
Home Front Memo. New York: Harcourt, Brace, 1943.
The Photographs of Abraham Lincoln, with Frederick Hill Meserve. New York: Harcourt, Brace, 1944.
Lincoln Collector: The Story of Oliver R. Barrett's Great Private Collection, with Oliver Barrett. New York: Harcourt, Brace, 1949.
The Family of Man. (prologue) with Edward Steichen. New York: Maco Magazine Corp. for the Museum of Modern Art, 1955.
The Chicago Race Riots, July 1919. New York: Harcourt, Brace and World, 1969.
Facts, Foibles and Foobles. Ed. George Hendrick. Urbana: University of Illinois Press, 1988.

BOOKS FOR YOUNG READERS
Rootabaga Stories, Part One. San Diego: Harcourt, Brace, 1922.
Rootabaga Stories, Part Two. San Diego: Harcourt, Brace, 1923.
Abe Lincoln Grows Up. New York: Harcourt, Brace, 1928.

Rootabaga Country. New York: Harcourt, Brace, 1929.

Potato Face. New York: Harcourt, Brace, 1930.

Prairie Town Boy. San Diego: Harcourt, Brace, 1955.

The Wedding Procession of the Rag Doll and the Broom Handle and Who Was in It. San Diego: Harcourt, Brace, 1978.

Rainbows Are Made. Poems, Ed. Lee Bennett Hopkins. San Diego: Harcourt, Brace, 1982.

Grass Roots. San Diego: Harcourt, Brace, 1998.

FICTION

Remembrance Rock. New York: Harcourt, Brace, 1948.

WORKS ABOUT CARL SANDBURG

Callahan, North. *Carl Sandburg: Lincoln of Our Literature.* New York: New York University Press, 1970.

Corwin, Norman. *The World of Carl Sandburg: A Stage Presentation.* New York: Harcourt, Brace and World, 1961.

Crowder, Richard. *Carl Sandburg.* New York: Twain, 1964.

d'Alessio, Gregory. *Old Troubador: Carl Sandburg with His Guitar Friends.* New York: Walker, 1987.

Detzer, Karl. *Carl Sandburg: A Study in Personality and Background.* New York: Harcourt, Brace, 1941.

Fetherling, Dale, and Doug Fetherling, Eds. *Carl Sandburg at the Movies: A Poet in the Silent Era 1920–1927.* Metuchen, N.J.: Scarecrow Press, 1985.

Golden, Harry. *Carl Sandburg.* New York: World, 1961.

Haas, Joseph, and Gene Lovitz. *Carl Sandburg: A Pictorial Biography.* New York: Putnam, 1967.

Niven, Penelope. *Carl Sandburg: A Biography.* New York: Scribners, 1991.

Sandburg, Helga. *A Great and Glorious Romance: The Story of Carl Sandburg and Lilian Steichen.* New York: Harcourt, Brace, Jovanovich, 1978.

Steichen, Edward. *Photographers View Carl Sandburg.* New York: 1966.

Sutton, William. *Carl Sandburg Remembered.* Metuchen, N.J.: Scarecrow Press, 1979.

Swank, George. *Carl Sandburg: Galesburg and Beyond.* Galva, Ill.: ` G. Swank, 1983.

Yannella, Philip R. *The Other Carl Sandburg.* Jackson: University Press of Mississippi, 1996.

SOUND AND VIDEO RECORDINGS OF CARL SANDBURG'S WORK

Carl Sandburg Reading Cool Tombs and Other Poems. Caedmon, TC 1150

Carl Sandburg Reading Fog and Other Poems. Caedmon, TC 51253

Carl Sandburg Reading From His Novel, Remembrance Rock. Caedmon, 1970

Carl Sandburg Reading "The People, Yes." Caedmon, TC 2023

Carl Sandburg Sings America. Everest, PS 309

Carl Sandburg: A Lincoln Album. Caedmon, TC 2015

Carl Sandburg Reading at the Joint Session of Congress, Feb. 12, 1959. Spoken Arts, 806

VISITING CARL SANDBURG SITES

Carl Sandburg State Historic Site, 331 East Third Street, Galesburg, IL 61401. This is the three-room cottage where he was born on January 6, 1878. The house, maintained by the Illinois Historic Preservation

The three-room frame house on Third Street in
Galesburg, Illinois, the birthplace of Carl Sandburg

Agency, reflects the typical living conditions of a late nineteenth century working-class family. Many of the furnishings once belonged to the Sandburg family. In a small wooded park behind the home is Remembrance Rock, beneath which Carl and his wife are buried. The staff can guide you to a dozen other places in town—schools, college, work sites—that figure in his early life. Hours: open daily nine A.M. to five P.M. Closed New Year's, Thanksgiving, and Christmas days. For further information write: Site Manager, 313 East Third Street, Galesburg, IL 61401, or phone (309)342-2361.

Carl Sandburg Home: National Historic Site. It is located in Flat Rock, North Carolina, twenty-four miles south of Asheville, North Carolina, and thirty-nine miles north of Greenville, South Carolina. Sandburg lived here from 1945 to his death in 1967. The rooms are as the Sandburgs left them, with books and personal items scattered about. The visitors' center, in the main house, has exhibits, films, a bookstore, information, and ticket sales for the house tour. You can explore the park area, see the farm buildings, the goat herd and dairy developed by Mrs. Sandburg, and walk the five miles of trails in the forest or on the mountain. From early July to mid-August the Flat Rock Playhouse presents *The World of Carl Sandburg*, *Rootabaga Stories*, and *Sandburg's Lincoln* on the park grounds. The park staff provides programs such as music, poetry, and cheese-making demonstrations during the summer and fall months. Open daily from nine A.M. to five P.M. except on Christmas Day. For further information write: Superintendent, Carl Sandburg Home National Historic Site, 1928 Little River Road, Flat Rock, NC 28731-9766; or call (704)693-4178. You may find information about the park at http://www.nps.gov/carl/ on the Internet.

INDEX